DATE DUE			

UNDERSTANDING
CATHOLIC
MORALITY

UNDERSTANDING
CATHOLIC
MORALITY

ELIZABETH WILLEMS

A Crossroad Herder Book
The Crossroad Publishing Company
New York

1997

The Crossroad Publishing Company
370 Lexington Avenue, New York, NY 10017

Copyright © 1997 by Elizabeth Willems

Printed in the United States of America

Library of Congress Cataloging-in-Publication Data
Willems, Elizabeth, 1937–
    Understanding Catholic morality / Elizabeth Willems.
      p. cm.
    "A Crossroad Herder book."
    ISBN 0-8245-1725-3 (pbk.)
    1. Christian ethics – Catholic authors.   I. Title.
BJ1249.W495 1997
241'.042 – dc21   97-28872
                                 CIP

CONTENTS

INTRODUCTION

One evening several years ago I was approaching my house, returning from a meeting. I slung my purse over my shoulder and walked to the door, when I suddenly felt a jerking and pulling at my side. A young man came from behind me and snatched my purse. Knowing I could not recover the purse, I yelled at him, "That's wrong. That's wrong." Later I was amused that, in the midst of anger and confusion, the moral theology teacher in me came to the fore and instructed the man about morality.

One does not have to be a moral theologian to say of some actions, "That's wrong." Most of us have experienced morally wrong actions and have done our share of them. If we have not experienced moral wrong ourselves we have but to watch TV or read the newspapers to see it graphically displayed. We may find ourselves saying, "That's wrong." Today's media seem to thrive on publishing the moral wrongs of individuals: rape, murder, drug abuse, sexual promiscuity, and marital infidelity. The media also show how individuals collectively contribute to society's evils through growing poverty and unemployment, cut-throat competition in the marketplace, ruthless individualism, unbridled greed, irresponsibility and infidelity in relationships, declining sexual mores, and business mismanagement. This book will deal with moral wrongs and will attempt to fine-tune the reader's assessment of moral wrong, but it will do so by focusing on the positive side of morality.

Powerful though sin is, it does not have the final word. Sin is really powerless in the face of Jesus, the compassionate Lord of all, who shows us how to live a virtuous life. Through the example of Jesus, the grace of the Spirit, and the guidance of the church, we can be strong in the face of evil. The writers of scripture and later the bishops of Vatican II, drawn to this God-Man, sought to keep the life and works of Jesus alive through their writings. In scripture and the documents of Vatican II, we learn the heart and mind of Jesus Christ and how to live his life today. The entire goal of Catholic moral theology is to put on the mind and heart of Christ. This book strives to enlist our heart and mind in living the moral life and in making moral decisions. The goal, *to put on the mind and heart of Christ,* is woven into each chapter, for it is only through this goal that one can understand moral theology. Moral theology understood in this way does not simply involve learning moral theory, doing right actions, obeying authorities, and earning points for heaven. Moral theology directs us to a right relationship with God, with others, and with ourselves. It requires a change of mind and heart based on the mind and heart of Christ.

Moral living, then, is more than simply doing right actions as taught by our parents, teachers, and society. Some "right actions" may be "politically correct" or polite but lack the quality of moral life characterized by a disciple of Jesus Christ. We do not refrain from stealing because we do not want to get caught, be punished, and lose our reputation; rather, as Christians, we do not steal because we respect the property of others and love them as we love ourselves. We do not associate with members of a minority race because they serve our economic and social goals; rather, we associate with all as colleagues, neighbors, and friends because each is equal and worthy in the eyes of the Lord. We do not downsize and lay off workers simply and primarily to keep a financial lead; rather, we strive to educate workers and keep them in the job market because it is just. We have responsibilities to workers because they are made in the image and likeness of God. Christian morality penetrates our mind and heart so that morally right actions emerge from personal conviction.

Each chapter will treat one aspect of the moral life. Conversion of heart and mind — the goal of moral living — is the focus of chapter 1, which presents a brief overview of medical, social, sexual, and business ethics. From this foundation, we direct our attention in chapter 2 to the person of Jesus, who is the norm of the moral life. The life of Jesus shows the importance of human beings in the eyes of God. In chapter 3 we examine freedom, the critical cornerstone of the moral life. The role of the faith community is laid out in terms of its use of freedom, responsibility, and moral decisions. Chapter 4 is a study of the human person and person-centered morality. Once a Christian anthropology is established, we can proceed to chapter 5, which deals with the human reality of evil and sin. Chapter 6 shows where the disciple can turn for moral guidance and treats the role of moral authority in the church. Chapter 7 discusses the role of conscience and its formation as well as the process of moral decision making. Chapter 8 shows how the moral ills of society today have strains similar to societies of the past. Historical study reveals the moral wisdom of our foremothers and forefathers and ways they chose to resolve moral conflicts. As our own church of today faces contemporary moral dilemmas we see efforts at renewal rooted in scripture and the early Christian community. Chapter 9 examines new movements in moral theology that are concerned with contemporary issues in moral living and decision making.

The thrust of this book emerged from my teaching and study of moral theology. I believe that through teaching moral theology, I have truly learned it. My first debt of gratitude, then, is to my students at Notre Dame Seminary: men now ordained, those preparing for the priesthood, and lay students, all of whose lives have helped ground my study of moral theology. Their idealism, interest, and reality-checks have given me the impetus to probe the discipline of moral theology, which is bottomless in terms of wisdom, peace, and love.

I am especially grateful for the support of a number of other people. Through the director of my thirty-day retreat, Vince Hovley, S.J., I came to "relove" the person of Jesus and to relearn the formative role of liturgy for the spiritual, intellectual, and moral life of discipleship. Without the vote of confidence from the rector, Bishop Gregory Aymond, whose life exemplifies compassion and commitment, my work at Notre Dame Seminary would not be possible. I am grateful to Reverend Richard Sparks, C.S.P., for his careful editing of my text, and I credit him for its increased worth to a wider audience of readers. The thoughtful and critical reading of my manuscript by Cletus Willems, Dr. Michael Duffy, and Dr. Colette Stelly were inestimably helpful for both content and style. The invaluable suggestions and support of Reverend Franz Graef, Dr. Gregory Vall, Marie Garon, and Reverend Paul Philibert, O.P., are greatly appreciated. I am grateful, too, to my community, the School Sisters of Notre Dame, and to my friends, colleagues, and family members, whose interest, love, and friendship enable me to see the work of God unfolding in all of God's works, including my own life. In these people I see the mind and heart of Christ.

Chapter 1

CONVERSION

The task of *Understanding Catholic Morality* is to explore how to follow Jesus Christ. It is a matter of putting on the mind and heart of Jesus Christ, loving as he loves, and thinking and deciding as he would. This book shows that to follow Jesus — to put on his mind and heart — is not a simple task. It takes a lifetime of commitment and continual efforts at conversion of mind and heart. To be a Christian disciple, one must be open to the teachings of Jesus and to the application of those teachings by the church. Conversion means learning to love as Jesus did, with the faithful, forgiving, accepting, and encouraging love he showed the people he encountered. To do this, a conversion of heart and mind is required, and this is accomplished only with faith. This chapter will address conversion and its call to individuals and the church.

Call of Faith: to Self and Community

Faith is a gift and a call. Belief in God, in his son, Jesus, and in the Holy Spirit is a gift of God's grace. Once that gift is given, it is felt as a call from deep inside and penetrates every part of our being. It enlivens our lives with new energy and gives us a new perspective on life. Faith gives us the perspective of Jesus.

The eyes of faith enable us to see and assess moral questions, issues, and dilemmas as Jesus would. Too often moral decisions are made from a nonfaith stance that relies solely on common sense and a pragmatic viewpoint that does not always do justice to those involved. It takes the deeper view of faith to work for justice and make decisions that are an "option for the poor." It is faith that enables a person to decide in favor of peace rather than arguments and fighting to solve a problem. Faith will take the way of humility in solving moral problems, rather than the way of dominance, pride, and self-righteousness.

Conversion encompasses more than an attitude. It is a way of being and a way of acting. All of one's life is turned around by the grace of faith that keeps calling one to turn to the ways of Jesus. The root word for conversion is the Latin verb *verto*, which means "to turn." Conversion is a turn *toward* Jesus and *away from* sin.

Conversion calls the believer to be a disciple of Jesus and to a kind of apprenticeship that trains the disciple in the ways of Jesus. The call is given personally and individually, through movements of the heart and mind. One person may experience a conversion of forgiveness and be able to forgive her father, who abused her for years. Another person may have a conversion of mind, which is then able to reason with faith and see why the church insists on service and justice for the poor and disenfranchised.

Individual movements toward conversion can be assisted through the faith community (the church), which is called to ongoing conversion. This means the community must continually examine the direction it is taking in following Jesus as a body, where the leadership of the Spirit is pointing, what the contemporary situations require of disciples, and how moral issues are to be addressed. In the faith community, members receive and celebrate the sacraments that call them to a closer union with Jesus.

Call to Conversion

Conversion to a moral life is a call to discipleship, to following Jesus Christ. Discipleship is a continuation of the call in Baptism and is reaffirmed in the sacrament of Confirmation. As one pursues the call of discipleship there will have to be a commitment to Jesus Christ that is accompanied by a moral conversion. The Christian commitment means one stakes all on Jesus Christ and his way of life. A commitment means there is no turning back but rather an anticipation of the future as better than the past because one has found the "right direction" with the right person. The right direction is the moral life based on the life and teachings of Jesus.

As a commitment to discipleship, the moral life is more than simply learning the right and wrong of morality, the legal parameters of society, or even the canonical boundaries of the church. A high school student achieved excellent grades in all areas of study, including religion. On the last day of school, she walked up to the desk of her religion teacher, took a scissors, and cut the A she earned for religion class out of her report card. She put the A on the teacher's desk, saying that was the end of religion in her life — the girl had misunderstood religion, had seen it as abstracted from the core of her being. Many people study the moral teachings of Christianity but are not committed to practicing them. Still others have been raised in homes where Christian moral values were taught and lived, but they have not made them their own. While intellectual knowledge and good examples are important to learning about Jesus, they are not the same as religion and not the same as faith, both of which require a commitment.

Conversion in the moral life means the disciple is principally committed to loving and knowing and serving Jesus Christ. Essentially, all conversions represent "turnarounds" in a relationship with a person and a turning toward commitment. For the disciple, the commitment must be made to a relationship with Jesus that is personal and real, not some theoretical relationship based on legalities and minimalism. A personal relationship with Jesus requires active faith and a prayer life that nourishes faith. A commitment to Jesus puts moral living in the realm of love that gives and forgives, that seeks justice for the oppressed, that strives for honesty in all areas of life, and that goes the extra mile of service. Without a commitment to Jesus, the disciple builds norms for morality that are impersonal and founded exclusively on reason, satisfaction, and pragmatism. We need to look to the roots of Christianity to understand what a commitment to Jesus and conversion can mean for the disciple today.

Morality of the Old Testament

Scholars trace the earliest writings of the Old Testament to the tenth century B.C. — to the Yahwist writer, the Succession Narrative, and the story of Joseph. For centuries, Christians have read these early stories and have seen the figures depicted in them as ancestors of our common humanity. Their struggles, fears, and joys are ours still today. From the pioneers in the faith we learn about moral living and about being faithful to a loving God.

What were the specific Judaic moral roots from which Christianity developed? Chief among them is the belief in one God, held so strongly by the Jewish faithful. At the center of all the Jewish moral codes is the Ten Commandments, the primary one being, "I am the Lord your God. You shall have no strange gods before me." This code was taught and retaught by the religious leaders of Israel.

The writers of the Old Testament describe the faith history of the

Israelites. It is a history of fidelity and infidelity: God is a faithful lover of Israel; Israel does not always return the love and at times falls short of the covenant agreement. The history of the chosen people is marred by sin and infidelity to the covenant, but it is also a glorious history of repentance and worship. With God's help and often at God's initiative, the people "turned from their wicked ways" and returned to God. The prophets were like shepherds who drove away evil influences, who at times chastised the Jewish leaders, and who exhorted the people to actions of justice and peace.

Several dimensions of Jewish Law, history, and practice guided moral thought and behavior. These included monotheism, the Exodus, the covenant, Torah, the Ten Commandments, communal bonds, and the role of the Law and prophets.

Monotheism and the Covenant

The faith of Israel was molded by the belief that there is only one God. Abraham (ca. 1800 B.C.), the ancestor of the faith, led the Israelites to a new understanding of monotheism. His pledge of faith in one God shaped the Jewish belief system. The experience of slavery in Egypt and the Exodus (ca. 1250) forced the Jews to confront and reconfirm their belief in God as well as their trust in God's provident care. Through dramatic signs the Jews were led out of slavery into the desert, where God spoke to and through their leader, Moses.

In gratitude to their gracious God, Israel forged a covenant that was declared by God with these words: "I will be your God, and you will be my people" (Exod. 19:5-6). The covenant was a bond of the heart. Faithful love was to be given to one God, the God of Israel. As pledge of this love, the Israelites accepted the Ten Commandments and pledged themselves to their observance.

The importance of the covenant cannot be overestimated in the faith history and moral development of Israel. Lest Israel forget its importance, the covenant of Sinai was renewed at critical times in its history (1 Kings 8; 2 Kings 23:1-3; 2 Chron. 34:29-31). Later the reading of the covenant was required every seven years at the Feast of the Booths (Deut. 31:10-13). Torah embodied the internal and the external realities of the covenant that ordered all of Jewish life: observance of the Law in a spirit of love.

It is quite evident that religious practice was not isolated from politics and social relations in the early formation of the chosen people. Once the chosen people entered the Promised Land, monotheistic faith posed political and social problems besides religious ones. Contrary to their neighbors, who believed in many gods, the Jews had only Yahweh, and their tenacious belief in him set them apart from surrounding people.

The Israelites' monotheistic faith met with hostility from their neighbors, which led to wars and even to death, as seen in the death of the Maccabees. Moreover, when wars were settled with treaties, the spoils often included the harem of the conquered king. Each woman brought her own gods into the royal household. King David had many wives and concubines, while King Solomon had hundreds of wives and concubines (1 Kings 11:3); both kings tried to please and appease these women by allowing them to maintain their religious practices. Some of Israel's leaders strayed from their covenantal pledge and allowed polytheistic beliefs to undermine the monotheistic faith of Israel.

At those times, God sent prophets to correct Israel. The conflicts and sufferings of Israel were interpreted in the light of the covenant and the Law. They were seen as sent by God to purge the faith of Israel and to bring it back to a faithful love. At some of these times God was seen as comforting, as supportive, and as a God who forgave his people. At other times God was pictured as avenging and wrathful, chastising the people for their wrongdoing and infidelity.

Torah and the Law: Ten Commandments

The chosen people learned God's ways through their leaders and patriarchs, such as Moses, Abraham, and Isaiah, and through kings, including David and Solomon. They also learned God's ways through the observance of the Decalogue, that is, the Ten Commandments. This Law represented their love for God and for one another. It was an agreement of affection and will that embraced all of their lives. Social life, political activity, work, economies, personal mores, and, above all, worship and religious practices were governed by this Law. Israel's God was a faithful God who loved them with a steadfast love. Their God was ever-merciful and compassionate toward them but was also a God who expected them to show their love by observing the Law, the Ten Commandments.

Many prophets castigated the chosen people when the Law became merely a code of behavior and not a means to total conversion. The covenant with God was meant not only to dictate the behavior of Jewish people but also, more importantly, to shape their minds and hearts. They were a chosen people, specially loved by God. In this chosen role, they were to live a life modeled on the love God had for them.

Every aspect of Jewish life fell under the Law. The Law explained codes of right behavior, but there was a need for interpretation of the Law for different situations, places, and times. The rabbis produced a body of oral and written tradition of the Law that was embodied in the Torah. The tradition of the Law grew voluminous, including over seven hundred specific laws that the conscientious Jew was to follow. For a number of reasons, however, ordinary Jews could not obey all the laws. Some were illiterate and could not read the laws. Others could not obey all of the laws because they were not of the priestly class, a requirement for fulfilling some laws. The poor and the outcasts found it impossible to be Law-observant Jews because of their class and situation in life. With the development of such an extensive legal system to govern the moral life, the purpose of the Law was lost because the hearts of the Israelites were not turned to God. Again, prophets were sent to bring the Israelites back to a right observance of the Law — not simply the letter of the Law but to a right loving relationship with God and with each other. Indeed, Jesus observed that some Law-conscious Pharisees of his day tended "to strain the gnat while the camel entered through the city gate." He meant, in essence, that the purpose of the Law had been lost due to the multiplicity of laws.

Justice

The Jewish people suffered injustice and discrimination in Egypt and in their periods of exile. They had firsthand experience of injustice. Their history of slavery, homelessness, wars, and exile made them sensitive to the poor, the suffering, the exiled, orphans, and widows. Care for each of these was written into their laws but more importantly into their lifestyle of social and religious practice. For example, the many wars caused the deaths of many able men, who left behind widows and orphans. The brother of the dead man was expected by law to marry the widow and care for her and her children. Widows like Ruth could by law follow the reapers and glean from the grain fields to feed their families (Deut. 16:19–20). The orphan, the widow, and the poor were specially dear to Yahweh. Therefore, justice for these groups was an important moral sanction in Israel. Because care for the poor and suffering of Israel was wed to worship, these unfortunates could go to the temple and expect to receive care. Each practicing Jew was expected to tithe money that maintained the temple and helped the poor of the nation.

Another favored group was strangers. Religious and social practice held that the stranger was to be warmly and generously welcomed. Abraham's welcome of the three angels disguised as travelers is a typical story of this welcoming behavior. A welcome to a stranger was a welcome given to Yahweh:

> For the Lord your God is God of gods and Lord of lords, the great, the mighty, and the terrible God, who is not partial and takes no bribe. He executes justice for the fatherless and the widow, and loves the sojourner, giving him food and clothing. Love the sojourner therefore; for you were sojourners in the land of Egypt. (Deut. 10:17–19)

"An eye for an eye, a tooth for a tooth" was a moral code that was practiced by some who did not balance justice with mercy. At those times, justice was meted out in ways that appeared to be vengeful rather than just. While the God of Israel was a God of justice, Yahweh was also a God wide in mercy, forgiveness, and compassion, virtues that the Israelites sometimes found hard to practice. In the midst of the cruelty of war and massacres, it was hard to be forgiving and compassionate, especially when they were defending their lives, their nation, and their holy places. Compassion and forgiveness could have appeared as weaknesses in the face of the enemy. It was then important that distinctions be made about upright behavior. The rabbis were charged with interpreting the Law in specific circumstances.

In all of Jewish history we read of Israel's longing for the Messiah who would deliver them. This longing was very strong by the time of Jesus' birth.

Morality of the New Testament

Jesus opened a new horizon for moral living — indeed Jesus was the new horizon! The New Testament writers record how Jesus lived and taught personal morality, the Law, community, and social relationships. Jesus' first concern was to fulfill the mission of his Father, whose message he came to deliver. Jesus was the full revelation of God as no other person or creature in the history of humanity. The impact of his revelation was powerful because it was given in a human person, "one like ourselves in all things save sin." Christ was and is a living revelation. While the Old Testament was replete with the stories of the moral failures and successes of the Israelites, it kept its vision on the future for the fullness of revelation. Jesus, as the Messiah, the fullness of revelation, lived with people in their daily lives; he showed the way of life that would lead people to eternal life and happiness. A road of spiritual and moral living was mapped out in the teaching and life of Jesus (a subject to be taken up in greater detail in chapter 2).

Both the Old Testament and the New Testament offer many avenues to conversion. They speak of faithful love, repentance for wrong doing, reverence for the Law, communal dimensions of moral behavior, and love as the basis for moral life. The scriptures exemplify conversion in all relationships — from those within a family based on kinship love to political relationships based on justice. While the scriptures map out routes to conversion, the disciple needs support, direction, and guidance in the arduous journey toward conversion of mind and heart. The follower of Jesus receives these guides through the faith community.

Sacraments of Conversion and the Liturgy

Each of the sacraments supports conversion to Jesus, but several give direct help in finding the new direction. When the sinner is alienated from self, God, and others, there is need for reconciliation. The sacrament of Reconciliation unites the repentant sinner with the various loves of his or her life and offers a means of turning away from sin to the ways of Jesus. While putting the sinner on the right path, it also supports the wavering foot that is insecure on the new way of conversion. The sacrament of Reconciliation affirms the sinner as one who is precious and loved. Sin is forgiven, and new horizons of hope open. This is a new day and there is a new tomorrow. No longer bound by the ties of evil, newly reconciled sinners know freedom of spirit as never before. They are free to be their true and best selves.

Matrimony is an opportunity for a conversion of love. By committing oneself for life to one's spouse, one enters a way of faithful love that is like the faithful love of God for the church. Conversion in marriage is far-reaching, for it touches every aspect of the couple's being and spirit. Two people now work together as a community rather than as single people acting for their personal gain and satisfaction. Because each person must consider the spouse when making decisions, each must constantly speak with the other, especially as they build a family. Thus married love daily calls the couple to conversion in their ways of thinking. Conversion of heart means love is expanded to include children, in-laws, family members, neighbors, and work colleagues. No longer seeking convenient ways out of interpersonal tensions, the married person now faces relational problems motivated by love and is willing to work through the problems with the spouse. Most of all the sacrament of Matrimony calls the couple to the kind of love that draws the two closer to each other and in turn to God.

Eucharistic celebrations also invite conversion. The Liturgy of the Word powerfully challenges the believer who listens attentively with an open mind and heart. Scripture is more than words printed in a bound volume. The Word lives in the believing community. Jesus' life becomes real when the gospel is proclaimed. The power of Jesus' life has inspired many to change their lives because some word of scripture has touched them. At the Liturgy of the Eucharist, Jesus nourishes the church with the bread and wine of his body and blood. The intimate union of the divine with the human effects a "turn" in the depths of believers because Communion brings us into the presence of God. Here we are known, loved, and accepted as we are. This personal union with God effects conversion of the mind and heart to Jesus. Besides the rituals of the Eucharistic celebration, the symbols and environment of worship move the heart to openness and prayer. Gestures, pictures, statues, crucifixes, incense, flowers, and music contribute to the atmosphere of prayer and conversion. The gospel choirs of the African-American community arouse people emotionally to praise and thank God. Community singing, choral music, and chant move other worshipers to a more sedate mode of prayer. Each mode of worship sets the stage for conversion of mind and heart.

Conversion is the call to union with Jesus. This union is promoted through personal encounters with the divine and through community experiences that enhance and nourish faith through liturgy, ritual, and the sacraments. Specific problem areas of society where Christian values are skewed or absent require conversion if evil is to be stemmed.

Values and Moral Conversion

The Sacredness of Human Life

Crimes of violence reported in the news and shown in movies make us cringe because life is not valued. It is cheap and easily expended with a gun, knife, or violent abuse. A USA Today headline read, "Polls

Show That Crime Is the No. 1 Issue in the USA" (July 18, 1995). The headline was part of a feature story that painted a new picture of the United States. "Afraid of crime, weary of incivility, many people are surrounding themselves with concrete and wrought iron and bathing themselves in bright, white lights. They're barricading streets, office buildings, neighborhoods, even parks. A people known for fiercely private and independent ethos are welcoming surveillance cameras and security checkpoints." When life is not reverenced, people become afraid. The numerous precautions taken by home owners, car owners, and others to create safety demonstrate the amount of fear people experience today because of crime and violence.

If crime is the number one concern of U.S. citizens, then conversion would mean respecting life as the number one value. Human life is precious from the moment of conception to the last breath. Jesus took on human life when he became one of us. In so doing, Jesus affirmed this life as good and as the way to union with God. Made in the image and likeness of God, human beings deserve respect and care. This is reflected in John Paul II's statement, "Man is called to a fullness of life which far exceeds the dimensions of his earthly existence because it consists in sharing the very life of God" (*Evangelium Vitae* 2). Simply being human is a basic criteria for respect that applies to all persons regardless of their age and race. When other criteria are used to determine the value of the human person, immoral situations develop. It is morally reprehensible to value another human being on accidental criteria like age, economic worth, color of skin, gender, intellectual abilities, or physical skill. The elderly person and the unborn, the poor and unemployed, people of color, women, those with marginal IQs, and the disabled must all be respected. If any of these marginalized peoples are demeaned by others, the value of life itself is diminished. No life is sacred as long as any life is not revered.

The Value of Earth and Property

Values bespeak what is esteemed, important, and desirable. We value what is precious to us. When human life is valued, then things related to human life are also valued. Two things related to the value of human life are the earth and property. The earth supports human life and provides an environment where people can make a living, can grow, and can find leisure. Because people are valued, their property is also valued. It is not surprising to find that in areas where human life is not valued, property and the environment are vandalized.

At one time vandals removed large planks in the Bonne Carré

Spillway, which keeps the water of the Mississippi River separated from the water of New Orleans's Lake Pontchartrain. The work of pranksters led to pollution of the waters through an overgrowth of algae that killed millions of fish and disturbed the entire ecosystem. Disregard and lack of respect for property and the environment affect the common good. Another example of disregard for the environment is the massive spillage from the oil tanker Valdez off the coast of Alaska. The incident ruined the coastline for years to come and caused the death of millions of birds and fish. Still another incident reported on a New Orleans newscast showed that the quality of human life and the environment were low priorities. "Fools! They are all fools! The city could have had millions of dollars if it would have allowed oil drilling in the lake," proclaimed an upset oil executive as he left a city council meeting. He did not get permission to do more oil drilling. The wise city council members heeded the warning of environmentalists and biologists whose concern for the environment won the day. This seldom happens because greed and economic gain often take an upper hand in convincing municipalities and states of the great financial boon they will have if more drilling and mining can be done.

The value of life must extend beyond the value of human life to include all forms of life. If human life is valued, then the environment of human life and property is valued. Only when there is a conversion regarding the basic value of human life and all aspects of life will the moral issues of crime and violence be solved.

Conclusion: Spirit Alive Today

"Ever-ancient, ever-new," the moral tradition of the church bears witness to the life and teachings of Jesus. To put on the mind and heart of Jesus is to "understand moral theology." Through the centuries, the Spirit has guided the leaders of the church, whose task is to apply the teachings of Jesus to each new age and to the unanticipated questions and problems of each age. While leaders and parishioners have made mistakes, and decisions sometimes have lacked foresight throughout the centuries, the moral tradition of the church has firmly upheld truth, wisdom, and basic moral values. The church has been committed to the pursuit of truth. Scholars, theologians, and pastoral ministers have implemented the best wisdom and truth available while seeking better answers to contemporary moral problems. They have sought to implement moral teachings in the compassionate and loving ways of Jesus through their scholarship, work, and ministry.

The Spirit has guided the church to formulate and uphold moral principles that honor the human person and society. Today's defense of the poor and the immigrant and the efforts for justice and peace and against war bear witness to the ongoing efforts of the church to stand on the side of "the least among us." History shows the strong stands taken by the church and its leaders in favor of moral good and in opposition to moral evil. Some leaders have given their lives, and others have suffered imprisonment and physical harm because they upheld the rightness of a moral position. There has been no want of martyrs and prophets for each age as it wrestles with its own moral dilemmas. The disciple is not above the master, and so the disciple may face some of the same painful encounters of the master, Jesus.

Discipleship and conversion of heart and mind are inseparable partners. One cannot be a disciple of Jesus without entering the process of continual conversion, an ongoing turning of the heart to greater love and of the mind to a more careful reasoning in faith. Unsettling and difficult as conversion may be, it is made easy through the Spirit whose grace assures us: "My yoke is easy and my burden is light."

Chapter 2

CHRIST, THE MODEL
OF THE MORAL LIFE

Have you ever been lost while driving in a big city? The freeway exit signs whiz by and add confusion to the insecurity about which exit to take. Many of us plan trips and try to ward off such confusion by studying a map and writing down directions or by calling a travel agent to send a detailed map. Even with such assistance, we may feel insecure because the territory is new. How much more pleasant to drive with someone who knows exactly where to go and which exits to take! Words, pictures, diagrams, and maps all indicate something, but they have to be matched with external reality to make us feel secure. We often find the best guide is a person who knows the way. In moral living this is also true. We feel most secure when others show us how to live morally. Influential people speak more by how they live than by what they say or write. Little wonder, then, that the best teacher of the Christian moral life is a person, Jesus.

In this chapter we will examine Jesus as the norm for moral living. His relationships and actions model the way of discipleship and can teach us today how to have his mind and heart as we face moral problems in our own social milieu. Jesus considered compassion to be a central moral category in dealing with the Law and social norms of his day. Jesus could be locked into history if we did not have his abiding presence in the Liturgy of the Word and the Liturgy of the Eucharist. We will explore the dynamic presence of Jesus in the Eucharist to see how it affects the dimensions of our own moral life and conversion. The liturgy is best seen in the context of the person Jesus, who through Word and sacrament models the moral life for us.

Person-Centered Morality

Jesus, a human being like us, is the model for the moral life, and he does know the way! All Christian morality follows this "person

model" to instruct us in the work of conversion and discipleship.
Jesus offers a lofty ideal, but his message is made concrete in human
beings living today. The methodology for moral learning given us
by Jesus is centered in individuals with dreams, needs, frustrations,
pains, worries, joys, and hopes. Jesus experienced these things, and
in dealing with them he modeled the moral life. His relationship
with the Father was person-centered, as was his relationship to his
parents, disciples, and apostles. Jesus taught by word and example,
using stories and analogies based on ordinary human life so all could
understand his message. He showed us that the most important
"word" is to live one's life morally.

Communication

Communication is the primary means of interaction between people
and an important means of learning. Parents teach values, beliefs,
and customs. These are taught on a person-to-person basis, chiefly
through communication and modeling. From the first days of life
when speech is still undeveloped, mothers communicate with babies
using not words but a "language" the baby will understand, "coos"
and "ahs." A glance, a smile, or a frown conveys meaning, through
which an infant learns that he or she is loved and valued.

Despite all today's technology to facilitate communication, often
the most impressive message comes in a gesture, a look, a smile, a
gift, or a touch. These too are "words." By his word, Jesus con-
veyed God's message to the world. If the gospel is the Word of
God, and Jesus is the Word, then communication is needed to spread
that Word. A person-centered morality, therefore, would include
communication and dialogue as core means to relay moral values.

As in the days when the gospel writers tried to transcribe Jesus'
life through words, so too, in this time, we learn of the man Jesus
through the treasury of scriptural words that portray Jesus as human
and divine. The words create images that disclose the moral values
and convictions by which Jesus lived and which he taught. Several of
these word-images are significant for morality because they spell out
how we are to be disciples of Jesus today.

Jesus in the New Testament

In a poem entitled "Step on It," Luci Shaw sees Jesus as a bridge
who shows us how to reach our dreams of "ambitious soaring" for
happiness:

All these broken bridges —
we have always tried to build them
to each other and
to heaven. Why is it such a
sad surprise when last year's iron-strong
out-thrust organization, this month's
shining project, today's
far-flung silver network of good
resolutions
all answer the future's questions with
rust
and the sharp, ugly jutting
of the unfinished?
We have miscalculated every time.
Our blueprints are smudged.
We never order enough steel.
Our foundations are shallow as mud.
Our cables fray.
Our superstructure is stuck together
clumsily
with rivets of the wrong size.

We are our own botched bridges.
We were schooled in Babel
and our ambitious soaring
sinks in the sea.
How could we hope to carry your heavy glory?
We cannot even bear the weight
of our own failure.
But you did the unthinkable.
You built
one Bridge to us
solid enough, long
enough, strong enough
to stand all tides for all time,
linking
the unthinkable.[1]

While we do not have a road map printed for every step of our journey, we do have a person to show us the way to travel. The road
for moral living is mapped out in the teaching and life of Jesus, who

was the revelation of the Father and the source of a morality of love, forgiveness, healing, and compassion.

Jesus: Revelation of the Father

Jesus' mission was to reveal the Father. The clarity of his mission was evident in his teachings about the Father, particularly in such parables as that of the Prodigal Son welcomed by the father, the Good Shepherd who sought out the Lost Sheep, and the man who gave the neighbor a loaf of bread. When Jesus fed the hungry multitudes, he acted like a nurturing parent. Like a compassionate parent, he accepted sinners and forgave the repentant. The poor and the outcast found a place in his social circle. His mission of revealing the Father laid the foundation for morality based on a renewed image of God: a compassionate, loving, and forgiving God. If the God that Jesus revealed is compassionate, loving, and forgiving, then all believers in this God and all disciples of Jesus must appropriate these same attitudes.

Jesus was able to carry out his mission because he knew the Father. The task was difficult. All his efforts to reveal the Father met with confusion and misunderstanding, even from the apostles. "Lord, show us the Father," pleaded Philip, to which Jesus replied, "Have I been with you so long, and yet you do not know me, Philip? He who has seen me has seen the Father" (John 14:8–9).

The message of union and communion was hard to accept because it challenged the disciples' conception of God. Jesus knew the Father in a personal, immanent way. The apostles, in contrast, had a more distant, transcendental image of God. Legalism had become the norm of morality. Jesus taught a mature and responsible love that reconstituted the nature of our relationship with God and with our fellow humans. Followers of Jesus were to accept all as brothers and sisters. Inclusivity was to be practiced.

The message of union and communion found expression in Jesus' everyday relationships with the apostles, the crowds who followed him, and the friends who cared for him. The respect Jesus showed these people laid a foundation for Christian social ethics today.

Morality of Love and Forgiveness

Jesus practiced the Jewish faith tradition while restoring and amplifying its lost or undervalued elements. This is particularly true of the Torah and the Commandments. The Ten Commandments represented the whole Law and enabled the fulfillment of the covenant.

By placing two commandments of love — drawn not from the Decalogue but from Deut. 6:5 and Lev. 19:18 — at the center of his teachings, Jesus taught a morality directed by love rather than a morality oriented by the Law. No longer could one argue from a legal perspective about moral right unless love of God, neighbor, and self was included in the argument. For example, some Jews hearing Jesus' teaching had difficulty with the concept of forgiving seventy times seven and of loving one's enemies. Legally, one was not required to do this. But true followers of Jesus took his commandments of love seriously and were willing to go the extra mile, continuing to extend love under the most difficult of circumstances. This not only met with resistance but defied common sense in the minds of some Jewish listeners. The same may be said of Christians today.

The poor, the sick, the outcasts, and sinners challenged Jesus' contemporaries. The legalists of the Jewish religion had relegated them to an inferior status in society and in religious membership. By accepting these groups of people, Jesus restored the teachings of the Old Testament to their pristine spirit of compassion. He also amplified and extended these teachings to lengths that some leaders in the Jewish religion could not accept. In fact, they judged Jesus to be a blasphemer, a heretic, and a nonobservant Jew who lived outside the boundaries of acceptable Jewish practice because he related to members of these marginal groups. However, these unfortunates saw in Jesus' teachings a place of moral rightness that validated their lives and their personhood.

Jesus the Healer

Many followed Jesus because his words affirmed them and gave them hope. They wanted to be healed. Jesus saw the spiritual illness that destroyed the spirit of the people he met. The diseases and illnesses had natural causes, but some spiritual maladies were due to immorality, to sins that harmed the soul and eventually the body and the psyche. As healer, Jesus cured illnesses of both mind and body; he restored people to full humanity. This meant they were able to carry out their duties of making a livelihood, parenting, and fulfilling their obligations in society. Once a healing was performed Jesus advised the person to "go and sin no more," thus illustrating the relationship between the spiritual and the physical, the psyche and the entire person. Jesus' healing ministry demonstrated that conversion includes the spiritual, the sociological, the psychological, the intellectual, and the physical.

Jesus the Compassionate One

> To complete the *imitatio dei,* to "be compassionate as God is
> compassionate," is to be like a womb as God is like a womb. It
> is to feel as God feels and to act as God acts: in a life-giving and
> nourishing way.... According to Jesus, compassion is to be the
> central quality of a life faithful to God the compassionate one.
> — MARCUS J. BORG, *Meeting Jesus Again for the First Time*

The core message of Jesus is to be compassionate as God is compassionate. Jesus translated God's compassion for us into human
terms, showing how we are to be compassionate with one another.
He showed compassion for sinners, the outcasts, the downtrodden,
the sick, and the marginalized of society. For these, Jesus had words
of care, understanding, and kindness.

The Hebrew and Aramaic words for compassion are based on
a root word meaning "womb"; they suggest both a feeling and a
way of living. Just as a woman feels compassion for the child of her
womb and as a person feels compassion for one who has shared his
mother's womb (i.e., a brother or sister), so followers of Jesus are
to be compassionate with others. The Greek word for compassion,
which is derived from the Greek verb *splagchnizomai,* which refers to
intestines, bowels, entrails, or heart, is used in the scriptural texts that
portray Jesus' closeness to the people. This explains the expressions
"he was *moved* with compassion"; "he *felt* sorry"; and "his *heart*
went out to them." Jesus experienced strong emotion for the suffering and the poor.[2] By contrast, the person who pities an unfortunate
person does so with little feeling or heart and is not moved by the
condition of the person. Pity is given by a superior to an inferior,
such as the pity we give the destitute and derelicts, the beggars and
homeless who are disdained. People offering pity cannot identify with
suffering people as brothers and sisters in pain but rather look down
on them as causing their own situation. Alms given in compassion
are given lovingly as to a family member in need; alms given in pity
are given detachedly to people who must be kept at a distance. Here
we see the importance of a moral attitude and character that incline
the disciple toward the heart and mind of Christ.

At Jesus' time some Jews had a legalist mind-set based on a purity
system. They regarded the unfortunate members of society with pity.
"You [Israel] shall be holy, for I the Lord your God am holy" was
translated into "You [Israel] shall be pure as God is pure." To imple-

ment a standard of purity, a system was devised to delineate between those who were pure and those who were impure. The system made judgments about purity and impurity in relation to five basic aspects of a person's life: birth, behavior, polarities, gender, and whether one was a Jew or Gentile.[3] Social boundaries were established based on one's purity or impurity: between the righteous and sinner, those who were physically whole and not whole, male and female, rich and poor, Jew and Gentile. Some examples might illustrate how the purity system operated. Tithing, the practice of giving a certain amount of goods to the religious institution, was expected on agricultural goods and was linked to purity in such a way that untithed produce was impure and could not be purchased by one who wanted to be pure. The pure person could not touch the impure one, as is demonstrated in the parable of the Good Samaritan: the man dying by the roadside could not be touched by the priest and the Levite because touching a dying, bleeding, or dead person would render them impure. Purity laws, rather than compassion and a person-centered morality, kept them from helping the dying man. Only one, the Samaritan, could assist the wounded man because he was already considered impure and was not bound by the restrictions of the Law. The Samaritan was free to offer compassion, to empathize with the wounded man. The morally right action for the Samaritan was compassionate action. Compassion was more important than the mere legalistic observance of the Law and reflected its true meaning.

Jesus established compassion rather than purity as a core value. This can be seen in the groups of Jewish society who were special recipients of Jesus' compassion. In the words and actions of Jesus we find consistent patterns of compassion and inclusion rather than exclusion. On many occasions, Jesus demonstrated how one is to feel and to be compassionate. He included the impure, the poor, and the sinners. The sick and handicapped were welcomed; parents were comforted when they worried about their dying children; widowed mothers were comforted; the hungry were fed, women among his followers were treated with equality and dignity. Jesus demonstrated compassion for all. Moreover, he frequently socialized with the undesirables of society — tax collectors, Gentiles, public sinners, the physically handicapped, and people possessed with demons — for whom few seemed to have compassion because it was thought they deserved their lot by reason of their impurity.[4] He dined with the impure, the socially excluded members of his society. Jesus' immediate circle of friends was hardly drawn from the politically well placed or the well-heeled members of Galilean society. Instead he chose his apostles from the lower class, the work-a-day laboring force of his time: fishermen and tax collectors. They were not the most educated or well-mannered men of Galilee but were a rather rough and uncouth lot whose hearts were drawn to this man Jesus. From his patterns of socializing and from his choice of apostles, we learn of Jesus' compassion for excluded groups of society.

Jesus' parables dramatically reinforce images of compassion. Through them, readers are oriented to the mind and heart of Jesus. The parables of the Good Samaritan, the Good Shepherd, the Prodigal Son, the Lost Sheep, and the Householder and the Vineyard illustrate how Jesus separated treatment of sinners and outcasts from the prevailing social custom of his time. In this, Jesus established a moral attitude of paramount importance.

The sayings of Jesus provide further insight into the compassion of Jesus. While the sayings are difficult to interpret, their tenor illustrates the direction of Jesus' moral thought. This can be gleaned especially in reading the Sermon on the Mount from the gospel of Matthew, chapters 5, 6, and 7. In these sayings vivid images of the Reign of God disclose the mind of Jesus. The Reign of God would lead a follower of Jesus to practice justice, honesty, generosity, and right living. In the beatitudes (Matt. 5:3–11), Jesus broadens the contemporary norms for religious living and again highlights compassion as a criterion for holiness. The truly holy ones are the poor in spirit, those who mourn, the meek, those who hunger for righteousness, the merciful, the pure in heart, the peacemakers, and those who are persecuted. Forgiving others, loving enemies, and treating women with dignity are all requirements for discipleship. Again, we see that Jesus' approach to people highlights the importance of compassion as a foundational moral attitude for all who want to be his disciples. They must "put on" the attitudes that shaped Jesus' own mind and heart. Indeed, Jesus' stress on compassion would lead us to conclude that compassion is the measuring rod for all who want to live a moral life. Compassion is the attitude of a disciple, of one who has faith in Jesus. However, compassionate acts do not always bespeak a compassionate heart.

Faith and Christian Morality

Almost daily, newspapers carry pictures of and articles about philanthropists who donate huge amounts of money to worthy causes:

college tuition for needy students, parks opened for inner-city youth, renovation of homes for the poor, support for the arts, and payment for surgeries on poor children. These magnanimous sharings of riches are in the spirit of Christ. But the widow who did not have great riches and who shared her mite (smallest coin possible) in the spirit of Christ was even more generous. Indeed, some philanthropists have ulterior motives for giving. An example is Henry, a well-known figure in a small town who decided to run for the school board. He was an agnostic, if not an atheist, yet he did not hesitate to take Communion during the Sunday liturgy, and he gave large sums of money to the church he attended. His reason: "I want people to see me as a religious man and so vote for me."

It is not the amount of the gift but the tenor of the heart that Jesus assesses. It is from the heart that the motivation for sharing with others springs. The followers of Jesus are invited to the high moral road of pure intention and generous sharing, all done out of love and faith, not for ulterior motives. Jesus chided those who gave money to impress others, unlike the widow who gave quietly from her meager funds. Some give gifts and services to impress others. Upright moral behavior that is only for show can be used for devious purposes. Upright moral behavior that reflects the intention of the heart and mind of Christ is true moral behavior. To live a moral life is difficult unless it has a setting that is encouraging, supportive, and sustaining. A vocation can provide this structure.

The Christian Vocation: To Follow Christ

A variety of vocations can support a commitment to Christ. The Latin word from which "vocation" is derived is *vocare,* which means "to call." A vocation is a calling to a state of life that emerges from one's inclinations and preferences for a way of life that will lead to wholeness and holiness. On the level of faith, a vocation enables a person to walk in union with Jesus and others and so arrive at union with God for all eternity. A vocation is the means by which a person follows a call from within and a call perceived to come from God to live a certain lifestyle that involves work, a given location, community involvements, and a circle of family and friends. These elements are included in a specific vocation or calling in life. The specific vocations of marriage, single life, or celibate religious life provide a moral setting that can lead a person to happiness and holiness.

The general vocation to follow Christ is shared by all Christians. This calling addresses the person in the depth of his or her being and touches all aspects of life. Disciples of Jesus follow his example and his teachings in the framework of a specific vocation where the general vocation of discipleship is enacted. Marriage is the specific vocation in which a couple accomplishes the teachings of Jesus in their relationship with each other and with their children. Single and celibate people carry the message of Jesus in their dedicated service to others. Celibates witness publicly to the love and care of Jesus for the poor and needy and in their service to the community of the church. Prior to Vatican II, the celibate state of life was considered *the* holy state of life; the single and married states were valued but thought to be inferior (*Lumen Gentium* 5). The bishops of Vatican II saw each state in life as a means to holiness and no state as superior to the other.

The general vocation to follow Christ is lived in discipleship similar to an apprenticeship. In the Black Forest of Germany, a tourist can visit the many shops where carved wooden sculptures are sold. Today many items are machine made, but one can still find some hand-crafted works, and these beautifully crafted items are prized for the skill of the sculptors who are able to carve delicate features into the wood. Tutoring under a master craftsman is required to master this art of wood carving. During the Middle Ages, a system of guilds existed to train aspiring young persons in the various crafts and trades. If a youth wanted to enter a certain profession, he was apprenticed to a master teacher. The stage of apprenticeship lasted from two to seven years and was followed by the journeyman stage. The apprentice would move into the home of the master teacher and learn the entire lifestyle of the craftsman, be he a wood carver, carpenter, wool dyer, bookbinder, or weaver. Only after years of extensive and arduous training could one hope to become a master or craftsman. The guild system was a model of discipleship, of formation, and of education in that the apprentice was a disciple of the master.

Jesus calls Christians to follow him and to enter into a lifetime of discipleship. "Following" today is often considered a passive activity and is thought to show a lack of initiative. This is not the case in true discipleship because it is an active type of following. One follows in order to learn the skills of the master. If the disciple is attentive, he or she begins to think like the master, takes on the attitudes of the master, and eventually acquires the ways of the master. Such is the vocation to discipleship with Jesus. It is freely chosen by the disciple, but once entered, it must continually be rechosen — for the disciple always has more to learn. Like the apprentice, the disciple will need the discipline of hard work, attentiveness, and responsibility. Though the task is difficult, the disciple learns the mind and heart of Jesus through prayer, the scriptures, and liturgy. In time, the disciple will experience a freedom of spirit. As the disciple embraces the Christian vocation, a fullness of humanity unfolds that brings peace, joy, and love.

Discipleship means taking on a new way of life that encompasses all of one's moral sensibilities. As one learns the mind of Jesus one begins to evaluate moral dilemmas with the mind and heart of Jesus. One begins to love and care and become responsible for people in the manner of Jesus. When these actions are done in faith, they reflect the moral stand of Jesus. The Christian disciple can give money to the United Way because everyone at the office is donating, but that same disciple can also give because he or she wants to help brothers and sisters in need. It is evident, then, that Christian discipleship encompasses more than performing moral actions — means becoming a moral person. The apprenticeship for a Christian disciple does not end with Christian education but is a lifelong enterprise of seeing in each new situation the concrete calling to respond with time, energy, material help, and spiritual support. H. Richard Niebuhr in his classic text, *The Responsible Self,* articulates this well in saying, "God is acting in all actions upon you. So respond to all actions upon you as to respond to his action."[5] Christian vocation is basically *a call to love and to put on the mind and heart of Jesus.*

The Call to Love: Basis of Christian Ethics

One of the most difficult challenges facing a Christian disciple is to love. Nevertheless, the Christian vocation is characterized by love. Love is the basic measure of the moral life, but not just any type of love is acceptable. The measure of love presented by Jesus is based on the two commandments found in Deut. 6:4 and Lev. 19:18: "The first is, 'Hear, O Israel: The Lord our God, the Lord is one; and you shall love the Lord your God with all your heart, and with all your soul, and with all your mind, and with all your strength.' The second is this, 'You shall love your neighbor as yourself.' There is no other commandment greater than these" (Mark 12:29–31). When God is loved first and foremost, then the second commandment follows as a necessary consequence because each person is seen as dear to God, the Creator. If God is loved, then it follows that every person must be loved.

What type of love is required to live a moral life? Jesus spells out the nature of the love he proposes through the use of parables and aphorisms. His love is forgiving, generous, inclusive, active, and radical. Jesus presents love as forgiving: one must forgive seventy times seven. That means disciples are to have a boundless love that continues to forgive repeatedly even when they are offended. This type of love challenges the disciple to a just love, a love that is active in calling into question injustices and wrongdoing but that forgives the wrongdoer. Jesus himself spoke words of forgiveness from the cross for the people who killed him: "Forgive them for they know not what they do."

Jesus presents love as generous: when a neighbor comes at an inconvenient time to beg for a loaf of bread, the good neighbor does not give a stone but whatever food is needed. When people are hungry, Jesus has them seated and provides a meal of loaves and fishes. Jesus presents love as inclusive and encompassing more than family. He poses the question, "Who are my mother and sister and brother?" and answers it by saying, "Whoever does the will of my Father in heaven is my brother, and sister, and mother." Jesus includes in his circle of friends and followers the Samaritans, sinners, the illiterate, the sick, and the poor. Jesus presents love as active: the parable of the Good Shepherd illustrates efforts to find the lost and those in need. The many healings indicate Jesus' active love that cares for people in their maladies, suffering, and pain. He understands the pain of loss and so in active love raises the son of the widow of Naim, the daughter of Jairus, and Lazarus, the brother of Mary and Martha. Jesus presents love as radical: we are told to love our enemies. Love is to be extended to those who dislike and hate us or who might even harm us. Certainly this radical love was lived by the martyrs beginning with Stephen, followed by most of the apostles, and in following years, by hundreds and thousands of believers who died and still today suffer and die for their faith.

The type of love Jesus models as a measure of moral worth is strong and stable. It is not based on a fleeting feeling but rather on a faith-based conviction. The love Jesus asks of his disciples is a mature and responsible love. The disciple is not expected to love everyone with the same degree of intimacy. Some people are deserving of a more committed love, such as those bound to us by familial, friendship, and marital love.

Jesus uses his own love for us to demonstrate our worth and lovableness in the eyes of God. One of the most direct experiences of Jesus' love is in the Eucharist, which is a profound conveyer of ethical values.

Liturgy and the Moral Life

Besides the experience of God's love for us revealed in the Eucharist, we encounter God's love through personal relationships. Gifts are one of the ways people express their love for us. The corner knick-knack shelf in my office holds gifts from students and spiritual directees over the years. A carved marble post .from India, a ceramic shillelagh, carved ebony figures from Africa, a decorated box and cup from Korea — all evoke memories of their givers. Love is warmed as my eye wanders to the items that evoke the presence of the various persons. Greg, Brian, Suyapa, Therese, and Keun Soo come alive again in their gifts. Each person is a gift in my life. Memory has the marvelous ability to call forth a person through some reminder such as the gifts on my shelf. Memory fills simple things with life.

Besides memories of individuals whom we love, whole groups of people and nations can share and remember a common love. For example, in the musical *Evita,* we sense the intense love that a nation felt for Eva Perón; national celebrations honoring Martin Luther King Jr. remind us of the affection many held for Dr. King. Sometimes a piece of music, poetry, an object such as a photo, or words of a speech will bring a person to life in our mind. The gestalt of the person is present — we are moved by the dynamism of his or her spirit. We experience a similar dynamism during a liturgy. Simple things like bread, water, fire, and wine remind us of Jesus' life and the lives of his followers.

Liturgy employs words and gestures that recall important religious events and persons. "Do this in memory of me" bespeaks Jesus' desire to be with us enfleshed in the simple gifts of bread and wine. "They knew him in the breaking of the bread": the impact of a simple gesture opens the disciples' eyes to a full awareness of the resurrected Jesus seated before them.

"Do this in memory of me" does more than jog our recollection or bring Jesus to mind. Jesus is fully present with the words of consecration, "This is my body.... This is my blood." Jesus, as divine and human, is present in the Eucharist. Memory plays a significant role in the Eucharist. As a person, Jesus is kept alive through the scriptural writings and traditions of the disciples.

During the Liturgy of the Word, memory is refreshed and Jesus comes alive within each person listening to the readings. We visualize and hear Jesus as he speaks and acts in the scriptures. We see him touching the dead daughter of Jairus and hear him say, "I say to you, arise." And we can see an angry Jesus acting vigorously as he overturns money tables and shouts at the merchants selling goods in the temple.

When the community gathers, it remembers and celebrates the Great Thanksgiving for all Jesus has done, is doing now, and will do in the future. It celebrates in Word and in sign. We hold a common faith that is strengthened through the reception of the Word and the sacrament of body and blood. The symbolic actions endorse life just as Jesus' Last Supper and Passion were endorsements of life. For Christians, the Eucharist is an outward movement of giving our bodies just as Christ gave his body. This type of self-giving love is apparent when spouses give themselves to each other, when a tired parent rises to care for a child, when a nurse already burdened with many calls answers still another call. These examples testify to the core value of Christianity: giving one's life in love so others might live.

In the Eucharistic celebration this love is made concrete in the Consecration and Communion given as nourishment. Liturgical gestures and symbols are expressions of God's love for us and our response in love for God and for one another. If love is the measure of the moral life, then the Eucharist is the enactment of that love. The love of Jesus for his disciples compels him to join his own flesh and blood with theirs.

Communicants give "my body for you" as they leave the church and join their families, go on to jobs, or begin a day of celebration. We are Christ and bring his message to our part of the world, to every person we meet, and to every event we encounter. This total oneness with each communicant helps us realize the profound and mysterious level of Jesus' love: "[E]very liturgical celebration, because it is an action of Christ the Priest and of his Body which is the Church, is a sacred action surpassing all others; no other action of the Church can equal its effectiveness by the same title and to the same degree" (*Sacrosanctum Concilium* 7).

The level of God's love is profound and mysterious, and the Eucharist recalls the death and resurrection through which Jesus gave himself for each person. The measure of love is life itself when that is required. Martyrs like St. Stephen (the first martyr) and the recent martyrdoms in El Salvador (the four women missionaries, the Jesuits, Archbishop Romero, and countless others) speak of the courageous love that enables persons to give their lives for faith-founded convictions. Martyrdom is the ultimate price to pay for love and moral convictions. The measure of love for moral convictions is less dramatic in the lives of ordinary people who experience small martyrdoms each day. Their offering of life in love is found in the humdrum of boring and tiresome factory work, in constant demands mothers know while caring for young children, in the challenges professional people make against unjust economic and management structures at work, in the efforts of leaders who hammer out a better political plan to serve the common good. Each courageous stand the disciple takes to uphold a moral conviction is a death to self and exacts its price. Sometimes the toll is loss of a job, loss of a friend, alienation from family and neighbors, or loss of standing in the community. At other times the stand brings forth new life and hope through changes that are made. Only with faith in God's Kingdom here, now, and to come does martyrdom for one's beliefs make sense. Without the perspective of faith and love, martyrdom would be nonsense. With faith, the gift of self becomes the gift of love that strengthens individuals and communities because of its incomparable witness.

As in the death and resurrection of Jesus, the Eucharist raises the measure of his love to the ultimate level. The gift of oneself for another is the ultimate gift of love. In the Eucharist, Jesus gives the total gift of his life for us, his beloved; we have the opportunity to give the total gift of our life to God. This action of donation makes the Eucharist a celebration of love. The proper Eucharistic sentiment is overflowing gratitude for God's love manifested in Jesus, a gratitude for all of life so generously provided. If morality upholds values, then the Eucharist is the deepest manifestation and celebration of moral values, particularly the value of love. All dimensions of Christ's love unfold during the liturgy: selflessness, generosity, courage, witness, forgiveness, reconciliation, humility, praise, and gratitude. The Mass recalls the death of Jesus, the epitome of selfless giving for us.

Eucharist and Moral Development

In an article on the Eucharist and the *Spiritual Exercises,* Vince Hovley, S.J., describes four movements in the Eucharistic celebration: entrance, oblation, covenant, and union.[6] Each movement invites the

worshiper not only to a deeper level of closeness with the Lord but
also to a deeper level of moral growth and commitment.

The first part of the Eucharistic liturgy invites worshipers to enter,
to "take off their shoes", as they enter holy ground, a holy space, and
a holy time. Each person enters with her or his own life story of family, physical condition, and social situation. The liturgy begins with
an entrance rite as a preparation to "enter" worship. This is done
by reflecting on our sins and allowing ourselves to be judged by the
Word. It means confessing our guilt in sorrow and repentance and
entering a life of conversion. Conversion most often is not dramatic
but rather gradual and characterized by unnoticed, steady efforts at
change in all aspects of the self: attitudes, feelings, actions, convictions, beliefs. It is hard for little Susie to stop telling lies about her
brother or for Cathy to quit gossiping about her colleagues at work.
"Entering" also means we enter the liturgy with all that defines us:
work, play, family, friends, worries, politics, plans, and dreams. Terry
enters the Eucharistic liturgy with thoughts of his son in high school
who just made the football team and also thoughts of his daughter
who is becoming a rather rebellious teen. Janice wonders if she will
ever find a job, while Jack is still smarting from the finality of his
divorce. The environment of each one's life can become the circumstance for sin as well as the opportunity for virtue. "Entering" means
we allow the Word to enter us, the listeners, as it judges, challenges,
inspires, consoles, and supports us through the life and words of
Jesus. Attentive listening fosters moral conversion through the words
of scripture that shape our moral sensibilities, moral outlook, feelings, and thoughts. We "enter" the mind and heart of Christ through
the Liturgy of the Word.

Liturgy begins with a gathering of the community in a reflective movement inward. The second movement of the liturgy involves
moving out of self to Jesus. Here we are invited to offer ourselves
in oblation. The self-offering is symbolized by our gifts of bread and
wine. We offer all of our life to God from the smallest worry to the
biggest sacrifice.

The third movement of the liturgy is covenant. A scriptural term,
"covenant" refers to a binding agreement between two parties based
on their word and honor. God and the Israelites entered into a covenant of love that extends to each of us today. We are God's people
and God is our God. Conversion to a life of love encompasses the
movement of "covenant." This is found in the dynamic flow of the
liturgy—from self to God to others. Conversion is possible only be-

cause of God's covenanted love for the church and for each member of the church. "I will be your God. You will be my people" is demonstrated anew in each consecration of bread and wine into the body and blood of Christ. Once again the believer knows that God's love is faithful to the end of time.

The final movement, that of "union," occurs with the Communion, when one is enfolded in the infinite, unconditional love of God for each person. As chosen people, the community has new life to carry on the human work and life of the day, be it cooking meals, hopping a bus to the office, or patiently enduring the aches and pains that often circumscribe the life of a senior citizen. The life of a Christian is one of faith that sees in the ordinary encounters of the day the "stuff" of the Kingdom of God. In the procession of people back to their pews after Communion, one observes the ordinary folks, those neighbors and friends one sees often. These communicants are all loved by Jesus. Each is precious in the Lord's eyes and therefore worthy of respect, dignity, and care. But beyond the Eucharistic liturgy, one is united with all those family members, friends, and neighbors who chose not to worship in community. We are united with them in our search for unity, meaning, and identity. Communion establishes solidarity, a oneness in Christ that binds all to all.

"One in Christ" means no one belongs to a lower class or to a place of privilege, and all are valued according to the measure of love. As the procession of Communion continues to the pews, so it continues in the movement outward to the world as one leaves the Eucharist. "Go, you are sent" is the mandate to the community. Each worshiper is sent to carry the good news to the world. Alive with Word and image, with a refreshed sense of being loved, the disciple is empowered to walk in Christ's name. Each worshiper is enabled by love to work for justice, peace, authentic human development, and right structures. At the synod of bishops in 1971, the bishops addressed priests, saying: "The liturgy, which we preside over and which is the heart of the Church's life, can greatly serve education for justice....The liturgy of the word, catechesis, and the celebration of the sacraments have the power to help us to discover the teaching of the prophets, the Lord, and the apostles on the subject of justice."[7]

The Future Dimension of the Moral Life

The Eucharist empowers people to be missionaries in this world, but the movement inward and outward of the Eucharist connects them to the spiritual world as well. The spiritual dimension touches on our future, which is implicit in the present because our choices now determine who we will be in the future. With our free choice, we make God's offer of salvation our own. We as human beings have the freedom to say no and refuse the offer of salvation or to say yes and shape our future according to the mind and heart of Christ. Human beings live in a definite place and time and are able through freedom to shape history, which extends beyond the present moment. At the same time, what is created and decided today has ramifications for the future. So too, salvation is offered today as already given in the incarnation, death, and resurrection of Jesus but extends infinitely into the future.

The doctrine of life includes life here and life after death in heaven, hell, or purgatory. The "already and yet to come" aspects of our life can be understood, first, as knowing we are already redeemed and, second, as anticipating a future that holds our eternal redemption. These two aspects exist in a dialectic relation with each other, for one affects the other. How we live the moral life now determines our future for all eternity.

Josef Fuchs argues that because human beings possess freedom, each is responsible for creating himself or herself for all eternity while living in the present time.[8] Because the exercise of human freedom in making moral decisions has ultimate significance for the future, it is obvious that time bears sacred importance. It allows us "space" to determine our relationship with God and with each other. St. Paul advises that time must be used judiciously, prudently, and in accordance with Christ's standard of love (Eph. 5:16). Actions, whether virtuous or sinful, are important because they determine one's life for the future. An eternity of happiness in union with the God of love or an eternity of rejection is the result of free decisions made in time. Freedom, decisions, acts, and use of time are all factors that shape the present and the future. Life in the Kingdom here is connected to life in the Kingdom hereafter.

Conclusion

We have in Jesus the image of how to live the moral life fully. His stands were often contrary to those held by people in power. He socialized with outcasts and sinners, did not seek positions of power, and was interested in being true to God, with whom he had a personal relationship. Jesus' values still challenge our moral thinking.

Compassion and freedom are hallmarks of a disciple of Jesus. In faith the disciple chooses to follow Jesus and then chooses a specific vocation. Support for a life of compassion and freedom is found in one's vocational lifestyle and at the gathering of believers for Eucharistic celebration.

A person has the power to shape life and history for all eternity. The history that humans create through thought, decisions, emotions, and actions carries deep significance. Human life has eternal value because the life of Jesus gave it significance. In becoming human, God raised humanity to a level beyond the human. Freedom and its partner, responsibility, will be discussed in chapter 3, but here we can appreciate the enormity of personal responsibility for one's moral life.

Notes

1. Luci Shaw, "Step on It," in *Polishing the Petoskey Stone* (Wheaton, Ill.: Harold Shaw Publishers, 1990), 100. Jesus is the model of the moral life and a bridge for all human beings who want to reach God. Shaw captures the role of Jesus who is the Bridge, while we build "botched bridges" in our futile efforts to reach the divine.

2. See Albert Nolan, *Jesus before Christianity* (Maryknoll, N.Y.: Orbis Books, 1992), 35–36.

3. Marcus J. Borg, *Meeting Jesus Again for the First Time* (San Francisco: Harper, 1994), 51–54.

4. Ibid., 50–53.

5. H. Richard Niebuhr, *The Responsible Self* (New York: Harper & Row, 1978), 126.

6. Vincent Hovley, S.J., "A Rock to Build On," *Review for Religious* 53, no. 5 (1994): 774–80.

7. David J. O'Brien and Thomas A. Shannon, eds., *Catholic Social Thought* (Maryknoll, N.Y.: Orbis Books, 1992), 297.

8. Josef Fuchs, "Basic Freedom and Morality," in *Human Values and Christian Morality* (Dublin: Gill and Macmillan, 1970), 92–111.

Chapter 3

FREEDOM AND
THE MORAL LIFE

The evening news broadcast shows a man shackled to a gate: he has been taken hostage by terrorists who make his freedom a bargaining chip to obtain their goals. A young man, a drug addict, holds up a local store demanding what is in the cash register because he needs the money for drugs. A couple married only three years seeks a divorce because they feel confined by an incompatible relationship. All of these people deeply desire freedom.

Journalists cover the negotiations regarding the hostage as negotiators spend long hours devising the steps to obtain his freedom. A young man with a degree in education chooses to teach in inner-city schools because he knows education can enable young people to rise above the confinements of their environment. Married three years and facing problems at work and in their marriage, a couple seeks help to solve their problems, determined to work at their relationship. All of these people deeply desire freedom.

The two sets of scenarios can be found in almost every day's edition of the morning paper. However, there is a vast difference between the type of freedom being sought. The second scenario opens doors of possibility for greater freedom and growth, while the first scenario stifles freedom and growth. What type of freedom releases people to be themselves, and what is the illusion of freedom that binds us in webs of dependency foreign to our nature? Why do people choose the latter when they really want the former? These questions can be answered after we have investigated freedom, its meaning in social terms, and its meaning in moral theology. Since freedom involves persons and their development, we can perhaps more truly understand freedom if we examine it through the lives of people, particularly the life of one who was really free.

Free Person and Morality

An image for moral living is the free person. It is easy to recall the video messages from Terry Anderson, who was captured by Islamic radicals, and of a U.S. pilot downed in North Korea. People who knew both men doubted if their words were truly theirs. Only in freedom are words and actions our own. Only in freedom can words and actions shape us as we shape them based on our thoughts, convictions, and feelings. So, too, only when I am free are morals my own. Morality by its nature must be freely chosen; coercion and manipulation have no part in freedom. While morality is largely learned from others, it becomes our own as we mature and make free choices. A child takes on the ways of parents and teachers. Teenagers frequently look to their friends for identity, for acceptance, and for determining what is morally right or wrong. Only as children and teenagers mature do they accept as their own the moral values learned from others.

Jesus: Freedom Is Relational

To ground moral living in freedom implies that I am self-directed and can shape my life according to chosen values and goals. This is especially true of Christian morality because I can choose to accept the moral teachings of Jesus, not simply the theoretical hypothesis of some moral philosopher. However, more than intellectual assent to the teachings of Jesus is expected from me as a Christian. Rather, I am invited into a relationship with Jesus, whose whole way of life becomes my model for moral living. Like all relationships, the one with Jesus exists authentically when it is freely chosen. In turn, his teachings and way of life free me to grow continually as a person. But how does this happen?

The freedom Jesus brings is founded on love. As I experience love from another, I realize that my very self is attractive and lovable. A consistent pattern of love by parents, relatives, and friends enables a child to delight in simply being alive. Have you not smiled as you watched a youngster learning to walk buoyed up by adults whose words, gestures, and laughter encourage the child? As the child is lovingly supported, it experiments with its legs and strives to balance its body. To the delight of their elders, some children will thrive on the approval and show off their newfound skills by dancing and waving their arms to music. They delight in being alive. The same is true of freedom. When they realize the love God has for them as unique persons, they feel free to be the unique and attractive human beings they were created to be. Love frees them. When a person is free, there is no pretense but rather a simplicity like that of the child, who is attractive and disarming.

Freedom Leads to Integrity

Freedom grows when I strive to live with integrity in actions and relationships. If there is congruence in my interactions with others, between my thoughts, convictions, attitudes, and feelings, I can finally have oneness of mind, heart, and actions. This is integrity born of freedom. All of these demonstrate congruence between inner and outer worlds. We see integrity born of freedom in the worker who admits he made a mistake, in the student who raises a question in class about her confusion, in the public official who concedes he finds no solution to a civic problem, and in the parent who seeks help in raising an unruly teenager. Integrity is obvious in these cases because the person is living freely and is therefore able to be "at one" within the self. While we spend a lifetime trying to reach a full level of integrity, there are times when we meet people who are "one" in themselves. Sometimes, maybe only briefly, we are at one in ourselves. The sense of oneness within ourselves gives us freedom but also expresses the freedom we are living at the time.

Jesus was a man of integrity and freedom. He lived out the moral convictions and beliefs learned from his parents, the society of his day, and his religion. As he grew to maturity, Jesus developed his own moral vision that emerged from union with his Father and that was augmented by those societal and religious expectations he had learned. His moral vision was wed to his identity as a person: he possessed personal integrity. When there is a lack of freedom, there is a lack of integrity within the self. Like the captive Terry Anderson, who was forced to live out the expectations of other persons (his captors) and another system, people who are captive to external forces are not free to be themselves. Actions and all of life become a sham because these persons are motivated by their "captors." External forces, not a self-chosen internal source, control them. Where there is freedom to be oneself, there is a greater possibility of personal and moral integrity. Jesus' life demonstrates moral integrity because his moral convictions were congruent with his actions and words. Jesus did what he preached; Jesus practiced what he taught. Just as Jesus grew in maturity regarding moral integrity, so Jesus grew in freedom. However, Jesus' freedom was not marred by sin and evil inclinations, so his freedom transcended that of human beings. As in all human beings, so in Jesus, freedom and integrity are connected.

Personal integrity is seldom seen before adulthood because it takes the experiences of childhood and adolescence to form a self and to get to know oneself. It takes maturity to speak and act freely out of personal moral convictions. Anyone who works with adolescents will know that peer pressure is frequently stronger than personal convictions. Teenagers have the psychological task of discovering who they are and who they want to be. Certainly teenagers can have learned intellectually what is morally right and wrong, but until they have made these judgments their own, they are not morally integrated and free. Of course, many adults also lack integrity. Jesus found this when he dealt with the Pharisees, whom he compared to a whitened sepulcher filled with dead men's bones. These particular Pharisees were neither hot nor cold; Jesus said their lack of integrity was reprehensible. Jesus further stated that truth comes from the heart, not from the mouth. Moral convictions emerge from an integrity of the heart. The entire person is truthful, not simply words spoken as truth.

Followers of Jesus are invited to live freely and with integrity, like their leader. He attracted followers not by coercion or manipulation but by appealing to each person's fundamental desires for good, truth, and love. Freedom came from their inner desires. They wanted to be their best selves, to reach beyond the confining walls of their sin-tainted humanity to the integrity and wholeness Jesus offered. Instinctively they knew where to find freedom of spirit — it was in following Jesus. His teachings on love and forgiveness took them beyond the bounds of selfishness and revenge. Following Jesus took people beyond the bounds of class and nationality because he included all. The followers of Jesus were free to interact with people of any class or nation as their equal. Equality was an important aspect of the freedom Jesus preached. In his teaching on the Kingdom, all were welcome and no one lorded it over the other.

Laws Can Lead to Freedom

Another aspect of freedom is law. Jesus kept the Law. Many believe they lose freedom and are restricted because of laws such as minimum-age requirements to purchase liquor, traffic laws, and laws regarding mandatory insurance in order to operate a car. They believe laws bind and confine a person in terms of their choices and desires: they cannot do what they want to do. "A prohibition only points to the other paths as possibilities by removing, or better, forbidding entrance to the dead end. A prohibition is not coercion since it appeals to the freedom of choice of individuals without effectively hindering them from choosing the dead end."[1]

Civil law is meant to maintain order in society while religious laws direct people to right order with God. When civil laws are right and just, they preserve the common good and the rights of all citizens, promote harmony and right relationships, and enable people to live and move freely in their countries and cities. Indeed, freedom is served and preserved by just laws. Moral norms are meant to guide us on the paths of virtue. They free us to choose ways leading to goodness and away from ways that lead to evil and the binding, enslaving ways of sin. Jesus saw the laws, both civil and religious law, as freeing and constructive. In the scriptures, Jesus says, "I am the way." His life was the way to freedom and a pointer to God, a guide toward the way of righteousness. Walter Kasper writes about the freedom of spirit found only in Jesus Christ:

> Christian freedom is not acquired simply; and is not simply acquired. It is a freedom which Christ alone vouchsafed us; a freedom which is granted us (cf Gal 5:1–13); a freedom bound up with Christ, so that the man made free through it belongs really to Christ, as Christ belongs to God (cf 1 Cor 3:21–3; 6:13–20). The freedom grounded in Christ and determined by Christ is freedom for one's fellow man; freedom which takes care, and does not destroy, but builds up.... The yardstick of Christian freedom is the selfless love of God which appeared in Jesus Christ and which takes effect in Christians.[2]

Freedom ultimately allows us to strengthen our inner mettle by loving God and others and strengthens us to follow the law of the Spirit that brings us to full human development. St. Paul speaks of the law of the Spirit as that inner law that brings us into union with God. However, human laws are not always founded on the Spirit and do not always free the human spirit. Norms of Christian morality are paths to freedom.

Freedom and the Moral Life

Americans generally associate freedom with rights: "If I can exercise my rights, I am free." When we voice political views without persecution, worship in the religion of our choice, vote, work, and publish our views, then we enjoy freedom. Because many of these rights have been denied people in some countries at certain periods in history, the persecuted chose to emigrate to new countries where such rights were respected and upheld. This concept of freedom motivated the founders of the United States when they sought representation in government. It is also the freedom sought by others who have migrated to America because they coveted many of the basic human rights every human being should have. On December 10, 1948, the United Nations General Assembly passed the "Universal Declaration of Human Rights," which includes thirty articles that spell out human rights for every person. These articles show the necessary relationship between rights and freedom. Each article can be realized only in an environment of freedom, for human rights require freedom to exist. The introduction to the declaration states, "Whereas recognition of the inherent dignity and of the equal and inalienable rights of all members of the human family is the foundation of freedom, justice and peace in the world..." However, the exercise of human rights does not completely define freedom. Freedom has religious meanings in addition to civic understandings.

Freedom and the moral life are intrinsically related. One cannot consider the moral life without exploring the relationship between personal freedom and moral maturity. How is moral freedom different from the social and political concept of freedom? What role does freedom play in moral thinking and moral choices?

Growth and Freedom

"I want to be me" is the innermost desire of every human being. It expresses the desire to be "free to be me." Yet that desire is the most difficult to realize and perhaps the most thwarted of all human desires. It takes a long time for people to realize who they are because to be "me" is a fuzzy concept for many. Just as people mature through stages of psychological development so freedom matures with the newfound psychological strength each age presents.

Developmental psychologist Erik Erikson has outlined eight stages of human psychological development (see table 1). Each stage presents the opportunity for a person to resolve a conflict rising to prominence at a definite stage of growth and when the environment makes certain demands on the individual. As the tension between personal growth and societal expectations reaches a crisis point, the person can choose a maladaptive and negative way or an adaptive

Table 1
Stages of Psychosocial Development

Stage	Age	Crisis to be Resolved
1. oral-sensory	birth–1 year	trust versus mistrust
2. muscular-anal	1–3 years	autonomy versus doubt, shame
3. locomotor-genital	3–5 years	initiative versus guilt
4. latency	6–11 years	industry versus inferiority
5. adolescence	12–18 years	identity versus identity confusion
6. young adulthood	19–35 years	intimacy versus isolation
7. adulthood	35–50 years	generativity versus stagnation
8. maturity	50+ years	ego integrity versus despair

and positive way to resolve the crisis. Only with a positive choice does the individual gain new strength and achieve normal development. For example, teenagers are faced with the positive choice of identity and the negative choice of identity confusion.[3]

Confusion and Freedom

The task of overcoming identity confusion is exacerbated today because teens in First World countries have a vast array of options and innumerable images from which to make choices that will shape their self-identity. In the past, lack of education, financial limitations, and demands of an agrarian culture limited choices for young people. That is less true today. This is evident in the media, which are powerful tools used by young people to define themselves. The media present a wide spectrum of images that young people can "try on" by identifying with TV personalities, with movie and sports heroes and heroines, and with noteworthy or newsworthy citizens of the entire world. Some teenagers feel overwhelmed by the options and opportunities and are unable to make choices, so they resort to foreclose on a decision. Given sufficient money and time, they may try out many directions in terms of study and career until they settle for one. For example, they may find it hard to select one path of study in college because it closes the door on other avenues of study they find equally interesting.

Choices and Freedom

> When freedom is really understood, it is not the power to be
> able to do this or that, but the power to decide about oneself
> and to actualize oneself.
>
> — KARL RAHNER, "Man as Responsible and Free"

When one makes choices, one begins to define the self, and the self is
revealed in the preferences. Clothes are one way people make a statement about themselves to the world: the self is revealed through the
preference for jeans, dress shirts, sneakers, wing-tip shoes, dresses,
and so on. Choices help people know themselves. When there are
no clear and determined choices about basic areas of life, a young
person cannot channel energy into developing a self; rather, indecisiveness drains a person of energy because energy is spent in several
directions. A more focused perspective channels full energy in one
direction. Indecisiveness about self-identity sets a person adrift with
little ability to make commitments regarding vocation, choice of a
mate for life, and career. Too often this pattern can extend into
young adulthood and beyond. Witness the person who has had to
extend college years because of indecisiveness regarding a college
major, or the person whose résumé reads like a grocery list because
he or she is ever looking for the perfect job. Others find it difficult
to choose a marriage partner, so they move in and out of relationships in search of the one person who will enable them to say, "This
is who I am."

Making choices, while difficult to do, is important for personal
growth and for other areas of life as well. While making choices
facilitates growth in more mature levels of freedom, indecisiveness
leads to a "vaporous spirit," to a certain ennui and lukewarmness
described in the Book of Revelation: "[Y]ou are neither cold nor hot.
Would that you were cold or hot" (Rev. 3:15).

Choices and decisions are crucial to the moral life, for in the latter
one must choose between good and evil. Choices for the good lead to
growth in moral maturity and the spiritual life. To waver is perceived
by many as condoning evil by inaction. The ability to make choices
also affects one's growth in freedom. Freedom of choice is one type
of freedom and is essential to the exercise of a more basic freedom.
When freedom of choice is not exercised, it stalls development of
other levels of freedom.

In a classic article, "Basic Freedom and Morality," Josef Fuchs describes four types or levels of freedom.[4] There is no clear-cut de-marcation between the four types of freedom Fuchs outlines, for each is connected to the others. The first, psychological freedom, refers to the free selection of choices such as indicating preference for red rather than blue, following a schedule, or choosing a job. External acts such as truth telling and kindness and inner acts of free will are examples of this freedom. With psychological freedom, one ex-presses personal inclinations, desires, and preferences that disclose something of the self who is making the choices. The choices create part of the psychological picture of the person.

A second type of freedom is the moral freedom exercised by a person striving to lead a good life by choosing to act virtuously and to seek God as a final goal. Here Johnny decides to tell the truth rather than lie about cheating on a test; Alice does not join in the office gossip that defames her boss; and Carol spends extra time with her aged grandparents who are lonely.

Christian freedom, the third type of freedom, is exercised through the indwelling of the Holy Spirit, who leads us to renounce selfish inclinations and to choose things of the Spirit.

Fuchs's fourth type of freedom, basic freedom, relies on the pre-vious three. This freedom enables us to decide freely regarding particular acts and goals, and these decisions then determine our-selves totally as persons.[5] Basic freedom thus invokes the deepest level of the self, for it calls for a free and basic self-commitment to love. For the believer, ultimate love is God, who is the fulfillment of freedom. Basic freedom, then, involves the gift (or refusal) of the self in love to God; through this love of God we come to love others and the self. Basic freedom involves total self-commitment; it has to do with a concrete act done freely, with either surrendering oneself in love or refusing a surrender in love. The act of surrendering in love frees us to become who we were created to be. In loving we begin to enter the world of the other, to think and feel through his or her perspective. Selfishness yields to generous giving and magnanimity of spirit. To love and be loved are the fulfillment of a deep desire in human hearts, but this fulfillment is granted only to those who freely enter the door of loving relationships.

Fuchs realizes the inability of human beings to love perfectly. Being human, we are only capable of imperfect love and of a self-commitment that is incomplete, immature, and imperfect.[6] Because of this, basic freedom is not static but ever invites us to deeper levels of freedom and growth in love.

The four levels of freedom reflect and create the quality of one's moral life. Freedom of choice is used to strengthen love and to build practices of virtues — or vices, when love is rejected. Repeated choices integrate layers of one's being so individual acts meet with less resistance and strengthen patterns of behavior and thought. In turn, these choices and patterns shape the self. Parents hope that the child taught to thank someone for small gifts will develop a sense of gratitude and will eventually become a grateful person. Likewise the youngster who is allowed to be destructive may assume that property and things do not deserve respect. This could lead to patterns of destruction, to criminal offenses. The choices of children do not correspond to the depths of self-commitment in basic freedom, so they are not moral in the full sense but only by analogy. Unchecked, choices could lead to an evil way of life that comprises a total commitment of the person in basic freedom. For example, a lie regarding a minor detail can be told without expressing basic freedom — one's total self is not expressed in the lie because there is insufficient matter or evaluation of the act. We know that concrete choices are important because they lay the foundation, stone by stone, for a strong and free moral edifice. A person becomes a habitual thief after repeated acts of thievery. A murderer develops through small acts of cruelty and hatred.

The positive exercise of basic freedom requires full understanding of ourselves at the core of our being, an understanding that comes from a relationship with the Absolute who is God. In freely choosing to perform or not perform a certain act, we determine the intensity of our intention and the amount of total self-investment in this act. A transgression of a speed law while hurrying to work may express little intensity and self-investment regarding our basic intention to love. However, a planned, connived, and schemed act of revenge on a neighbor manifests more intensity regarding a nonloving intention. Because of the time given to planning the act of revenge, as well as the mental and psychological involvement, there is evidence of great self-investment. This could constitute a total act of self, an act of moral evil called mortal sin.

The amount of self-investment helps determine the self as a loving or nonloving individual, not just in time but for all eternity. The person who commits his or her life to loving God, self, and others will know total love in God for all eternity; the person committed to a life of evil will know the absence of love for all eternity. Grace, present in every situation of moral good, can be accepted or refused through the activation of basic freedom. This freedom integrates all aspects of the self toward its final goal of love, at which point one is truly free. When basic freedom is exercised in a choice to love, life energies can be channeled into a basic stance or orientation toward what is loving, good, and true. It is clear that freedom, so glibly discussed in political and social conversations, has deeper religious and moral meanings that engage the entire person at his or her depths. Freedom is more than rights — it is also responsibilities, particularly the responsibility to shape the self to truly "be me" and the responsibility to others in the community.

The Faith Community as a Guide to Freedom

> We live and move and have our being not in ourselves but in one another; and whatever rights and powers of freedom we possess are ours by the grace and favor of our fellows.
> — JOHN MACMURRAY, *Persons in Relation*

Disciples of Christ, sojourners on the road of freedom and love, must act freely. They must be conscious and reflective when acting; they must elect to love, for love is the environment and condition of freedom.

These are lofty ideals that are difficult to keep alive and act on alone. With others the ideals and their practice become realizable. The community of faith becomes the home base for disciples on their journey. Here the batteries of love and freedom can be recharged. Here stories are exchanged, confidences shared; discouragement yields to smiles; wisdom and guidance light up the way; and forgiveness heals wounds. These wounds can be deep enough that a person finds it difficult to love. Loving and attentive listening by a community member is one way to share the burden of another. No longer bogged down with the burdens of work, family, relationships, and illnesses, the believer finds ground for hope and is enabled to continue the journey more freely and with renewed love.

Christianity is a communal faith that informs the moral life. Individualism and isolationism are foreign to Christianity. "God did not create man for life in isolation but for the formation of social unity."[7] From the inception of Christianity, community life marked the relationship of Jesus with his disciples. He called apostles and disciples together and sent them out together. They prayed together, traveled and lived together. The early church kept this tradition of communal involvement alive as it worked out the specifics of faith and practice. Councils and meetings spelled out what the community would hold as true; never was this spelled out by one person alone. Individualism, the tendency to place the self at the center of moral decision making, flies in the face of the community of faith that is the visible body of Christ today. Not as self-styled individuals but as parts of the whole, all contribute to the life of the living community. This emphasis on community follows the ministry of Jesus, who operated with a community of disciples, and the apparitions of Jesus after the resurrection, which were given to the apostles gathered together. From these communal roots established by Jesus and carried forward by the apostles, the church has set its direction. It is a community of faith that discerns the leadership of the Spirit through the community. Vatican II took a firm stand in favor of community involvement in important aspects of church life and mission. Vatican II's document on education states: "Moreover, they [laity] should be trained to take their part in social life, so that by proper instruction in necessary and useful skills they can become actively involved in various community organizations, be ready for dialogue with others, and be willing to act energetically on behalf of the common good" (*Gravissimum Educationis* 1). The bishops of the United States have invited the active participation of the laity in every aspect of parish life, in diocesan synods, even in the writing of pastoral documents.

The church operates in several ways to develop community and to overcome present tendencies toward individualism, a tendency that in itself is a moral concern. The most important way to form community is through the Word of God. This Word is celebrated in the Eucharistic liturgy under Word and sacrament. Enda McDonagh, in *Invitation and Response,* argues that a Christian community is formed not by its members but through the Word or self-giving of God to all people that forms us into a community.[8] United in worship of the same God, nourished by the Word through the scriptures heard and then applied to our life and fed through the body and blood of Christ, members of the community share a common belief and a common purpose for being. We share the same mission of being sent to bring Christ to the world.

The church also assists its members by illuminating how to live the Christian life. Through spiritual helps provided in the sacraments, we are able to live the life of a disciple. Prayer, pastoral guidance, spiritual direction, and prayer groups support members on their spiritual journey. Moral norms provide guidance to recognize, know, and judge what is consistent with the mind and heart of Christ in today's world. Having a common moral understanding enables community members to be a force for good. Dialogue between members, clergy, and hierarchy keeps information about moral issues current and assists those who have to make moral decisions. The core norm of "love God above all things and your neighbor as yourself" becomes a living guide when community members reflect on its meaning in terms of the issue before them. Moral norms emerge from the community and are strengthened by the wisdom of its members. The weakness of individualistic outlooks is exposed as lacking the breadth and depth of perspectives that are more community-oriented. A communal perspective seeks what is good for all members when it pursues the common good. McDonagh believes that "whatever human activity then promotes this community is a correct response to God, morally good activity; whatever activity hinders or disrupts the community is a failure in response, morally bad activity. Community building becomes the criterion or norm of morality."[9] Community building is consonant with morality and receives the force of a moral norm.

These are significant concepts for the moral life. Freedom in Christ gives me hope that personal efforts to lead a moral life will be blessed and that the efforts of the church will be fulfilled. Knowing that God is present to support, assist, and motivate me through the grace of the community helps me realize that the life of a disciple is not meant to be a lonely one. The journey of freedom is traveled with other sojourners all seeking the same goal of freedom through love.

Freedom and Responsibility

> Let them form men too who will be lovers of true freedom —
> men, in other words, who will come to decisions on their own
> judgment and in the light of truth, govern their activities with
> a *sense of responsibility*, and strive after what is true and right,
> willing always to join with others in cooperative effort. Religious freedom, therefore, ought to have this further purpose
> and aim, namely, that men may come to act with greater responsibility in fulfilling their duties in community life.
>
> — *Dignitatis Humanae* 8

When a call has been given, there is an expectation of a response. The call to freedom requires a response; rights are matched with responsibilities. Each of the types of freedom requires a response. Moral theology studies freedom because of its decisive role in moral decision making. Basic freedom calls for a total response of the person, a response of a life of love or a response of a rejection of love, a response to seek the good and do justice and mercy or a response of no love, injustice, and lack of compassion.

Each type of freedom carries with it a call to respond that we call responsibility. Psychological freedom of choice carries with it responsibility for the consequences of our choices. When I choose to buy a car, I also choose the responsibility of paying for it and the car insurance. If I choose not to speak to a friend, I am responsible for straining the relationship and alienating that person. In moral freedom I can respond with a choice for the good, but when I choose evil, I must pay the consequences of evil choices: maybe guilt and shame, spiritual alienation from God, and less love in my relationships with others; possibly punishment or my own deterioration into self-hate. Social and political freedoms must be exercised responsibly. To remain politically free, citizens must be involved in their government, must vote, must defend their country, and must use and preserve freedom of speech, the press, and religion.

Basic freedom calls for a full response of the person to God, self, and others in love. The person who has reached a sense of self-identity knows something of the self as a person in relation to other persons, to the world, and to the social milieu. Karl Rahner would say that when we have this sense of self, we experience ourselves as subjects and are then ready to experience freedom and responsibility in the depths of our existence.[10] At this point of maturity, we experience the self as responsible and ready to stand boldly before others. We will also have experienced the Transcendent, which can be either accepted or rejected. We must then responsibly and freely interpret ourselves in terms of a self-commitment to love or to reject love, with grace to accept or reject the Transcendent. Human beings are free to realize the self or take a stand of self-refusal before God. We are free to say yes or no to ourselves and God.[11]

The responsibility of love permeates all of one's life. It calls for a moral response on a deontological level (the level of law) in the commandment, "You shall love the Lord your God with all your heart, with all your mind, and your neighbor as yourself." It also calls for a teleological (purposive or end-oriented) response to God who is the goal of our being. In God is our fulfillment as human beings, and in God is found fullness of love, happiness, joy, freedom, and peace.

Born into a human family, we are social beings. Human beings not only are social or communal by nature but are created with intense desires to love and be loved. The child needs and loves its mother; the mother has strong bonds of love for the child. Loving the other is built into our makeup, as seen in our attraction to people, our desire to know them, and our choice to be of help to them. We are responsible not only for those whom we love but also for our neighbor whom we do not know, particularly the poor and those in need. Jesus' teaching on compassion was highlighted in chapter 2. The scriptural narrative of Cain and Abel (Gen. 37:26) makes us aware that we are our "brother's [and sister's] keeper," contrary to the isolationist tendencies of those who are wealthy and powerful. Pope John Paul II writes:

> We cannot but think of today's tendency for people to refuse to accept responsibility for their brothers and sisters. Symptoms of this trend include the lack of solidarity toward society's weakest members — such as the elderly, the infirm, immigrants, children — and the indifference frequently found in relations between the world's peoples even when basic values such as survival, freedom and peace are involved. (*Evangelium Vitae* 8)

The pope outlines our responsibility to the many people needing our love, care, and concern. Disciples of Jesus lead a moral life when they live a life of love, justice, and compassion. Basic freedom calls the followers of Jesus to make such a response.

Basic Freedom

> Hence, in making a basic choice I commit myself as a person, I dispose of myself, as it were, and make myself good or evil as a person at my deepest level, in my heart.
> — WILLIAM COSGROVE, "Basic Choice and Basic Stance"

Basic freedom, as we now understand, involves more than simply making choices about what we prefer and choosing single acts for good or evil; it is the freedom fundamental to our existence as persons. The exercise of basic freedom involves deciding at the core of our being who we are now and will be for all eternity in relationship to God, self, and others. It is more than a choice for good or evil; it is a choice of how to live a moral life by committing ourselves to a life of love. This choice engages our total selves as working, social, playing, feeling, reflective beings.

Theologians have defined the total commitment of self as a fundamental option. William Cosgrove says a fundamental option is made at the center of the person using basic freedom. Because fundamental-option theory focuses on the core of the self and its growth through the stages of life, it takes account of depth psychology and developmental psychology.[12] The self is no longer defined by single, isolated acts but as a whole.

A fundamental option establishes my basic moral stance. It is moral because I choose it in full knowledge and freedom and am free to change it. Once the fundamental option is made, it determines my stance toward good and evil in terms of an orientation to reality, to life itself, to people, and to God. I decide to be a fundamentally good or evil person.[13] Cosgrove goes on to say that the fundamental option "takes place at the core of the person, at his deepest level of being, and it concerns a choice to be and become as a person, rather than to do anything or choose a specific object or value."[14] The fundamental option goes beyond all specific choices to do this or that and involves choosing to be rather than to do. However, the fundamental option is based on specific acts. Pope John Paul II in *Veritatis Splendor* clarifies this: The "fundamental option...is always brought into play through conscious and free decision. Precisely for this reason, it is revoked when man engages his freedom in conscious decisions to the contrary, with regard to morally grave matter" (67). Because the fundamental option is based on specific decisions, "the fundamental orientation can be radically changed by particular acts" (70).

Some life situations may clarify the fundamental option. From adolescence, Tom has known he would someday marry, but he wanted a woman who would share his ideas of married life, children, economics, and politics. Tom had maintained some religious beliefs and had tried to live a Christian life. Only after he landed his first job and was then laid off did Tom have to confront some harsh realities in life: scarcity of jobs, loneliness, and feelings of inferiority. Try as Tom might, no employer seemed to need him. This pain caused Tom to examine his motivations for working. Now that money was scarce, Tom wondered if he sought certain jobs and rejected others because he wanted to live luxuriously. This question made him realize he was considering only himself and not really looking at others. How was he planning to use his talents and education to help others? In his lonely dilemma his dreams for marriage also came under scrutiny. Did he want an attractive wife primarily to reflect positively on him, or did he want a wife who was valued for her own worth? Tom reflected on these and other questions. Because he felt powerless in the situation, Tom began to reach out to One more powerful than himself; he prayed. Eventually Tom made a grounded choice: he chose to commit himself to God in the trust that God would provide and care for him. He shifted the focus of his job search from concentration on the "good life" to include service through a job that provided a stable income while it used his talents and education. At the core of his being, Tom made a fundamental option for good.

Fuchs believes fundamental choices are made at momentous times in one's life: a tragedy such as the death of a dear one; personal illness; a decisive move toward married, vowed, or priestly life; a decision to enter the church. These times provide the opportunity to engage one's entire self in a fundamental choice for a life of evil or a life of surrender and generous love. Tom's outlook changed once he made a choice focused on the good; he was now ready to choose those acts, people, situations, and jobs consistent with his core decision. Tom's moral stance was directed toward the good.

Cheryl and Gary married just after both had completed college. They embarked on their separate careers and were quite well adjusted in their jobs. Although both had attended Catholic grade and high schools, neither had strong religious leanings or had attended church services since early college years. They had too many problems with church structures, and what happened in the churches seemed irrelevant to them. Then Cheryl became pregnant. They were excited about the child that would be theirs, and they dreamed of all they could give their baby. Their discussions led to questions of religious upbringing. To give a child religious values meant they themselves would have to practice their religion. They found a parish both felt comfortable attending and spoke with the pastor about their difficulties with the church. After baby David was born they attended the baptism classes that led both of them to take their religion more seriously and to examine the role of God in their lives. They decided to become involved in some of the parish programs. By the time of the baptism, Cheryl and Gary had reclaimed their religious roots in a more mature way and were ready to make a fundamental option for good, for God, for living loving lives as they reared their child. The occasion of the birth and baptism of their child provided the opportunity for this young couple to make a fundamental choice, one that had been prepared for through their years of schooling, their openness to embrace God in their adult life, and their desire to give David their best.

The fundamental option of a Christian involves a desire to be converted to Jesus. It says I want to become an active disciple whose entire life will be geared toward putting on the mind and heart of Jesus Christ. While this cannot be accomplished through a one-time act of the will, it can develop in ever-deepening levels through each stage of life. God's graces continue to effect conversion through the church and in daily events of life. The option must be reaffirmed and strengthened, as is done at each Holy Saturday renewal of baptismal vows where the community states its belief in Jesus and renounces evil.

Other means of strengthening one's commitment are the Eucharistic liturgy, sharing with members of the faith community, and personal prayer. Perhaps the strongest support of our fundamental option for love comes from the people closest to us: a spouse, best friend, children, family, and maybe colleagues at work. People who really love us want us to be our best selves and support us in drawing out our dearest desires and dreams for the good.

In addition to these supportive people, the church offers assistance to its members through its leaders and moral norms. Disciples are able to face moral situations with their own insight and wisdom gleaned from the believers who have gone before them in the faith as embodied in the tradition.

Conclusion

We have seen that freedom is more than rights and duties; it is at the core of a human being. In freedom we define who we are as persons. Each of us decides about what kind of a person we are morally and about our own personal development, the types of relationships we foster, our vocational choices, and most importantly our response to God's call to love. Our response will be evident in moral decisions and in the exercise of rights and responsibilities. Freedom is a prerequisite to the formation of moral character, for without it moral choices are not our own; with freedom we form who we are now and for all eternity.

Notes

1. Roger Burggraeve, "Prohibition and Taste: The Bipolarity of Christian Ethics," *Ethical Perspectives* 1, no. 3 (1994): 135.

2. Walter Kasper, *Jesus the Christ* (New York: Paulist Press, 1976), 157, 213ff., 223ff.

3. E. H. Erikson, *Childhood and Society,* 2d ed. (New York: Norton, 1963); idem, *Identity: Youth and Crisis* (New York: Norton, 1968), 94.

4. Josef Fuchs, "Basic Freedom and Morality," in *Human Values and Christian Morality* (Dublin: Gill and Macmillan, 1970), 92–94.

5. Karl Rahner, "Man as Responsible and Free," in *Foundations of Christian Faith* (New York: Crossroad, 1978), 35–39.

6. Fuchs, "Basic Freedom," 96.

7. Enda McDonagh, *Invitation and Response: Essays in Christian Moral Theology* (New York: Sheed and Ward, 1972), 53.

8. Ibid.

9. Rahner, "Man as Responsible," 37–38.

10. Karl Rahner, "The Theology of Freedom," in *Theological Investigations* (New York: Seabury, 1974), 6:178–96.

11. "Developmental psychology is the study of the psyche and its maturation through the various stages of growth, particularly as the growth is related to social and environmental influences. In psychoanalytic usage the term [*development*] is applied specifically to those growth processes directly dependent on interaction with the environment and through which the major psychic structures (id, ego, superego) form. *Maturation* refers to physical and psychic growth related to the inherent genetic potential and largely independent of external factors" (Burness E. Moore and Bernard D. Fine, eds., *Psychoanalytic Terms and Concepts* [New Haven: Yale University Press, 1990], 55, 56).

12. William Cosgrove, "Basic Choice and Basic Stance — Explaining the Fundamental Option," *The Furrow* (August 1984): 509.

13. Ibid., 510. See also Karl Rahner, "Original Sin," in *Foundations,* 106–15; idem, "Sin, Guilt, and Fundamental Option," in *Practice of Faith* (New York: Crossroad, 1983), 107–14.

14. See also Fuchs, "Basic Freedom," 98–104.

Chapter 4

THE MORAL PERSON

Skyscrapers, high-speed computers, the Internet, and massive and sleek bridges are master works of human beings. The beauty found in line and design, phenomenal feats of technology and scientific development, characterize these machines and structures. All testify to the intellectual and artistic abilities of the human being of the twentieth and twenty-first centuries. Just as daring and marvelous were the discoveries and developments of human beings in past centuries. The achievements of Marco Polo, Edison, Galileo, Joan of Arc, Dante, Madame Curie, Einstein, and Shakespeare testify to the timeless genius of human endeavor.

Human beings do not achieve knowledge or insights in isolation but as social beings living and working with other human beings. "We stand on the shoulders of those who have gone before us" is a maxim for researchers and for everyone wanting to live a fully human life. The scholars of each century stand on the shoulders of scholars from past centuries. Inventors, explorers, teachers, engineers, artists, and technicians reap knowledge and techniques from predecessors who share with them one basic thing: humanity. It is this that allows them to communicate knowledge to each other from generation to generation.

This chapter will look at humanity from several perspectives: the meaning of personhood; human beings as creatures; human beings as made in God's image, fallen but redeemed; the subjective and objective knowledge of self; the human with divine presence; nature and grace; a person-centered morality; the effects of human nature on our acts; and reason and will. There are many ways to approach this examination of humanity, or anthropology, but most helpful for our study of the moral person is a theological approach. This chapter, then, will show the importance of the human person in terms of Christian morality.

The Meaning of Personhood

Human beings share a common humanity. We cry and laugh at events; we toil and struggle to reach our goals, to raise our children, and to become good at our jobs. What is common to human beings is often what is found in the ordinary, everyday lives of people and shared events of daily life: tiredness at the end of a work day; worry about bills getting paid; stress created by illness; concern about children; joys in achieving a goal; happiness in the love of a child, a friend, or a spouse; belief in more than is here and now. Consider:

- *A human being is* a woman who gives birth to a child in the dark night while her husband fights in one of the numerous ethnic wars spawned after the collapse of communism.

- *A human being is* the young man named Bill who just completed his education and was newly employed in a firm that offered many opportunities for this talented young man. Now Bill fights the debilitating effects of AIDS.

- *A human being is* Terry, an African-American twelve-year-old who lives in the St. Thomas housing project of New Orleans. His father abandoned the family, and his older brother was shot when a drug deal went bad.

- *A human being is* Mae, an elderly woman in a nursing home who is fearful of life and unable to make her body, and now her memory, respond to her desires. Lonely and depressed, she faces each day with less hope than the preceding day.

- *A human being is* the congresswoman facing a tough decision about voting for a bill that contains facets contrary to her moral beliefs but that has financial benefits and programs for the needy people of her district.

- *A human being is* the young woman who just delivered her first baby, tired but ecstatic with the newborn she and her husband already treasure.

- *A human being is* the unborn fetus a mother carries even while she decides if she wants to continue its life within her, the decision made difficult because she does not have the means to care for the child.

- *A human being is* the wealthy woman in a mansion with antique furniture, oil paintings, and exquisite appointments that distinguish her as a woman of upper-class status.

- *Human beings are* all of those many ordinary folks — undistinguished, facing moral issues, but faithfully discharging their family, civic, and religious duties. When we study moral theology we are studying about the lives of these people. They are the mail carriers, car mechanics, students, sanitation workers, nurses, and grocery check-out clerks we see every day. They read the morning paper, hurry off to work, listen to the 5:30 news, watch sports, take their kids to practice, and hope their monthly paycheck will cover family expenses this month.

All of the human beings mentioned above are unique, ordinary, and share a common humanity. Their physical builds, ages, personalities, genetic traits, personal histories, and environments make them unique. In their uniqueness they are "precious in God's eyes" because they were created as singular individuals to reflect God's creative newness. These people are ordinary in that they share basic traits with other human beings: basic physical needs for food, shelter, clothing; basic psychological needs for belonging, love, social relationships, attention, security, and self-esteem; basic religious or transcendental needs for meaning, hope, and fulfillment of ultimate desires. These desires for complete love, happiness, peace, and joy, St. Ignatius of Loyola calls "the more." Most people are ordinary like the people listed above; however, these persons are also incomparable, interesting, and unique in their personalities, character, and appearances. All of them have the "stuff" of holiness in their ordinariness. John W. Donohue, S.J., observes there has been

> a shift in the saint-making process: a shift from a concentration on priests and religious to a greater recognition of the heroic virtues of lay persons and an emphasis on the truth that holiness consists not in spectacular achievements but in the performance of life's common duties uncommonly well as a way of loving God in practice.[1]

This shift is evident in the men and women John Paul II beatified while visiting several Asian countries in 1994. Peter To Rot from Papua, New Guinea, was a married man chosen for beatification. When the daughter of Blessed Peter To Rot was asked if her father had any extraordinary religious experiences, his daughter replied,

"He was extraordinarily ordinary."[2] By simply being an ordinary human being, one can share life to the fullest with the divine. To realize the profound depth of this reality, one is led to ask, What does it mean to be an ordinary human being? and How can a human being come to share life to the fullest with the divine? Moral theology deals with the commonalities of human beings, their uniqueness, and their potential for holiness as creatures of God.

Persons are Creatures

> The nature of man consists above all in his being a person (i.e., possessing *ratio*). Nature is not understood as human, unless it is thought of as a *personal* nature....It would be possible and perhaps more meaningful to speak of "person" as a moral norm instead of "nature"...man is essentially person and has to understand himself therefore as person — "in a human nature" — and achieve self-realization according to self-understanding.
>   — JOSEF FUCHS, S.J., "The Absoluteness of Moral Terms"

A human being is first of all a creature of God. As created and not the creator of ourselves, each of us has limitations by the very nature of human life. Within ourselves, we are dependent on the divine for life itself and for every breath and movement of our bodies. No person could live one minute without a proper balance in the cosmos between land, air, sun, and water. This state of dependency on other human beings, on the natural environment, and on God does not detract from the dignity we have as human beings but rather establishes an order of being. The human person is created in relationship to a higher being who created the universe.

When I was a child I would lie on my back on a summer's evening to see the wondrous sky lit with zillions of stars and planets. The sky was awesome with the grandeur of God's creation. Seeing the starry heavens was one of my first encounters with God as Creator. While the sight filled me with admiration of God, it did not draw me close to the Creator because God seemed so distant and beyond me. I wondered how a God who created the stars and planets that were so far beyond my ability to comprehend could care for me personally. Besides, I was only one of millions of human beings created by God. This view of God was amplified as I grew older and encountered painful events that could have been attributed to chance or could have been caused, or at least "allowed," by God. All of this made me wonder about God's love and care for me and for all creatures.

The Israelites, too, wondered about God's involvement with creation and particularly with human beings. Israel was God's chosen people, yet the Israelites experienced great pain, sorrow, and loss. Did God care for them? They experienced the earth as parched from lack of rain followed by famine and pestilence. We know of hail storms that stamp out fields that were to yield a harvest for people and animals. Is this the work of a loving Creator? The Ice Age ended an entire civilization. Forest fires level thousands of acres of wooded land. Floods and landslides wipe out whole cities and ruin the homes of numerous people. Wars often bring devastation and death to innocent people. These realities raise questions of faith for us and questions about the divine. Can a God who permits these disasters be a provident, loving Creator? The ordinary persons like Bill, Terry, Mae, and the pregnant woman mentioned at the beginning of this chapter face important moral questions whose answers are interwoven with their belief in God. All of us likewise must contend with similar questions at some time in our lives.

The scripture writers pondered these same questions about creation and the Creator. Scripture reveals a loving God who drew very near to the chosen people, who cared for Israel in the desert, and who helped them establish homes in the Promised Land. No people had a God as close to them as God was close to Israel. The scripture writers teach us that the Creator-creature relationship can be based on love and trust that generate great freedom, initiative, responsibility, and interdependency. A loving God provides what is needed for creaturely life to thrive and trusts human beings to be self-determining and to use earthly resources well. A provident God, the scripture writers say, has an intimate love and care for every creature, for each creature reflects God's goodness.

Consider how the Creator's goodness is evident in the creatures surrounding the human person: the morning song of the meadow lark, the repertoire clearly sung by the mocking bird, and the curt chirping of the cardinals. Squirrels run up and down trees while dogs bark their zealous interest in the squirrels' every move. Cats comfortably stretch in beguiling ways to have their heads scratched and to get food. The panoply of colors found in forests and flower gardens all over the world suggests beauty that is original in each blossom and a mystery in each bud unfolding before the sun's light. "Sky-shows" of bold and subtle colors at sunrise and sunset over the mountains bedazzle the reflective spectator. Rain, sun, winds, soil, and seeds, under proper conditions, provide the vegetation that nourishes people and animals and protects the earth.

The earthly ecosystems, a concern of environmentalists and ecologists, are the magnificent creation of a provident God who cares for creatures. Moreover, this earth is entrusted to us creatures to exercise our own provident care for it and to exercise our own creative energy in using its resources. That is one sign of a balanced relationship: people use their own creativity to care for others and to let others be themselves. In a dependency relationship, one person cannot exist without the other but must rely on the other to define who one is because one does not have a sense of self. Not a dependency relationship, the Creator-creature relationship calls for maturity and responsibility; it calls for a fundamental characteristic of all healthy relationships: active trust in self and trust in the other.

When we consider the creation of man and woman, we see God's hand at work. The beauty of the human person is remarkable. For centuries, artists and sculptors have tried to capture the marvel of the human body in their works. Hollywood and modeling agencies develop astonishingly beautiful photos and films of women and men. While not everyone has an attractive, well-proportioned body, human beauty can also be found in the attitudes, beliefs, actions, words, and personalities of people. There is beauty in children. All of us have seen the delightful innocence of a child who affectionately hugs daddy or mommy and sees the world afresh in the events of each day. There is beauty in the youngster eagerly and earnestly trying out a new skill. One cannot but admire the child who shares lunch with a needy person, who offers help and comfort to one who is upset and crying. The mother and father who spend wakeful hours caring for a sick baby are beautiful in their loving care and concern. The generous gift of self is evident in parents who sacrifice their resources, time, and energy to nurture their children. People who forgive someone who wronged them have a special vibrant and strong beauty. Those who care for the sick and elderly are attractive because of their gentleness and dedication. Strong beauty is found in those who speak for justice, who take stands that improve the structures of society. One could think of those people down the block — neighbors, relatives, teachers, mentors, clergy, acquaintances, and even strangers — who have done things or said things that have moved one's spirit to admiration, generosity, and wonder. Every person is beautiful in his or her own way and at his or her own times. All are precious in God's eyes because of their marvelous creation. Although human beings have the potential for beauty and the development of a loving nature, the fact is all of us are affected by original sin and participate in what is ugly and unloving. We have a dark side that is evident in our sinful ways. However, the innate worth of human beings, whether sinners or saints, is determined not by their looks, talents, or performance but by their creation in the image of God.

The Human Being as Made in the Image of God

A human being is a wealthy woman in the mansion with antique furniture, oil paintings, and exquisite appointments that distinguish her as a woman of upper-class status.

The Creator-creature relationship exists from the moment of conception, and there is a likeness to the Creator in each person. Some people, like the wealthy woman, locate the source of their worth in created things and in the recognition of people rather than in the Creator-creature relationship. We are made in the image of God, which is the true source of worth, although we are different beings from God and do not share the same nature. Because we share in the life of our Creator, human beings have a bond of closeness with the Creator unlike bonds between creatures. Parents see and experience the similarities between themselves and their children: "He is just like you"; "she has your eyes." On physical, intellectual, psychological, and many other levels, children are similar to their parents. In the child, parents see something of themselves. In some relationships, such as between a parent and child, there are bonds stronger than death. Comrades in arms, friends, relatives, and some relationships of care and responsibility also have ties that powerfully bind one person to the other. But the Creator-creature relationship — grounded in the presence of the image of God in human beings — is on a deeper level than even the relationship between a parent and child. The level is a spiritual one that embraces the indefinable mystery of a human being. Made in the image of God, human beings share a spiritual nature that penetrates all levels of their being and weds them at their core to each other and to their Creator.

In what ways does the human person "image God"? As a human being I am first a be-ing rather than a do-er. This definition is quite recent, considering that "person-as-doer" and "person-as-agent" have been the predominant definers of human beings. In Scholastic

thinking a "human" is defined by what he or she can do and produce. Some described this view with the title "Man the Fabricator,"
emphasizing that a human being can use intellect and muscle to make
things, can dominate the earth, and can change things for the con-
venience and necessity of human beings. Building highways, planting
crops, cutting trees, erecting buildings, designing and assembling cars
are evidence of "Man the Fabricator." While that characterization of
the human person is true and worthy, there is danger that persons
might be valued only for what they produce and not for who they
are. If the dignity and value of a person is defined by what she or he
does, then many people would be considered "valueless": the elderly,
the infirm, infants, the mentally and physically challenged. The mystery of people extends far beyond actions and words into the very
being of human creation. The final definition of human worth is that
each person is made in the image of God. Later we will see that the
retrieval of virtue and its place in the study of ethics demonstrates
this shift in moral thinking from emphasis on what one does to who
one is. The following example demonstrates the shift.

Tom got a ticket for speeding because he was preoccupied and did
not notice his speed. The ticket and disobedience of traffic laws do
not define Tom as a person, for the person who is Tom remains after
the ticket is issued. Actions reveal something of the person — speeding reveals that Tom can become preoccupied when he is worried
about something. Actions such as driving a car proceed from one's
interior thoughts, emotions, and desires and do express a person, for
as moral theologian Timothy O'Connell says, "I do, the person that
I am."[3] Our actions are not separate from us because actions em-
anate from the core that is the self and express us. Tom's actions
express him and shape his personality and character, and, indeed,
Tom shapes his character and personality by what he chooses to do
and be. Repeated actions become habits that shape the person who
is Tom, but the worth of Tom's existence is basically defined by his
Creator, not merely by his actions.

Subjective and Objective Knowledge of Self

Another aspect of the self is subjectivity. Tom cannot stand back
and see himself as person — his self cannot be objectified. The self
is nonreflexive and subjective. Tom can see the traffic ticket he received because the ticket is an object outside himself; but Tom cannot
see himself as an object. Tom can know something about himself

through what others tell him: how he looks, how his words and actions impact others, how he measures up in comparison to other people, but Tom cannot get outside of his own skin to observe himself. Tom can make other people the subject of his observation, but he cannot do that to himself, and so he cannot get an objective view of himself. Tom's knowledge of himself is quite subjective, tempered with some objective knowledge. We are reliant on others to help us know various dimensions of ourselves: intellectual, physical, psychological, spiritual, social.

The social dimension of the self is revealed through interactions with others and through relationships. In relationships where people can be themselves, their true feelings, motives, desires, and dreams can be shared and are a window to the self. A parent knows the child after living with him or her for many years. A close spousal relationship allows each to know and be known by the other. A person is revealed most easily in trusting and committed relationships such as friendship and marriage. However, persons are mysteries even to themselves and consequently to others.[4] The image of God that marks all persons is partially revealed through the self but is always beyond full revelation and expression. Just as God transcends all human categories, so the life of God that exists in human beings is not able to be fully objectified. We have signs of God's life in us, but we do not have absolute objective certainty. The reality of God's life transcends our ability to know.

•

A *human being is* Mae, an elderly woman in a nursing home who is fearful of life and unable to make her body, and now her memory, respond to her desires. Lonely and depressed, she faces each day with less hope than the preceding day.

On some days, Mae's smile reveals that love and hope are still alive. The staff at the nursing home and visitors fan the flame of hope in Mae. We see glimmers of the Transcendent in all of creation, including human beings like Mae. Artists and writers like William Shakespeare have tried to capture this throughout the centuries. In *Hamlet,* Shakespeare marvels at the abilities of human beings:

What a piece of work is a man, how noble in reason, how infinite in faculties, in form and moving, how express and admirable in action, how like an angel in apprehension, how like a god! (2.2.303–7)

The Human with Divine Presence

Theologians struggle to express what seems inexpressible about the divine image found in human creation. Some writers describe glimmers of divinity. They call God "the nameless one" or "the silent one" who is always there but who can always be overlooked, unheard, and passed over as meaningless.[5] Such glimmers can be found within ourselves when we feel interminable desires, hopes, and yearnings for more love, peace, joy, and fulfillment. We can see the most breathtaking sunset and wish it would last; a love relationship can reach a peak of mutuality that unites two people, but this exquisite moment ends, contrary to our desire to have it go on for all eternity. History shows that the rich and powerful always want more than their mansions, money, and jewels can give. According to St. Ignatius Loyola, our desires exceed human boundaries and so reflect our deepest desire for God.

Besides "touching" God in our deepest desires, we can encounter the mysterious presence of God in "limit-situations" such as death, extreme pain, alienation, loss, great loves, and tremendous joys.[6]

•

A human being is Terry, an African-American twelve-year-old who lives in the St. Thomas housing project of New Orleans. His father abandoned the family, and his older brother was shot when a drug deal went bad.

Although a young boy, Terry knows poverty, tough living conditions, loss, and pain. Just as our desires take us beyond what human and earthly things can satisfy, so painful situations like Terry's take us beyond the intellectual and emotional patterns of our ordinary life. These occurrences take us to the limits of our capacity to experience and endure. Our intellectual limits drive us to question what we do not understand. The limit-situation is frequently expressed in the simple but profound question, Why? And very often we cannot answer the question but spend our lives searching for an answer.

Some of our desires do not reflect our desire for goodness, truth, and God. While our deepest and most authentic desires reflect our desire for God, human desires can also be devious and evil. Our quest for "the more" can show itself in our quest for power, accomplishment, recognition, possessions, beauty, comfort, and luxury. Self becomes the center of the universe, and others become a means to achieve our selfish goals. Things become tools to accomplish our devious desires that indeed exceed human boundaries.

Our desire for God is stronger than our inclination toward sin because of the power we possess through the redemption. Our desire for God is evident in our efforts to capture complete love, goodness, beauty, peace, harmony, truth, and justice. When a person takes the time to reflect, the strength of these desires can be felt and known. During a recent thirty-day Ignatian retreat, I had the time to examine the basic spiritual drives of my life. Although it took some time to dust off the superficial drives of my busy and involved life, it was surprising to find that my strongest desires were ultimately for God. This is experienced by most retreatants because all people share this drive for the divine. Masters of the spiritual life, like St. Ignatius of Loyola and St. John of the Cross, recognized this and built spiritualities on the human need for transcendence and "the more." These innate desires of the normal human person could be called interior signs of redemption. The church offers a means to find redemption through worship and the sacraments.

What do these abstract concepts of self, "the more," and "limit-situations" have to do with moral living? Moral theology is concerned with the core of a human being, with the self. Conversion, discussed in chapter 1, is aimed at the core level of a person's being. It invites one to "turn from" and "turn to" at the core level of self. If conversion has as its only goal the changing or termination of actions, that can be accomplished through punishment, rewards, or behavior modification. However, those efforts do not change the core of the person.

A teenager, Keith, who is caught shoplifting, receives a stiff punishment under the law and is punished by his parents. Keith may try to avoid shoplifting, but there is no guarantee he is no longer a thief. Terminating behavior does not mean that the self has changed. Conversion changes one's heart, relationships, attitudes, and way of thinking about life. Conversion hopes to capture the core of the person and direct it to the potential for fullness of self found in Jesus Christ. It encompasses all expressions of what it means to be a person: actions, relationships, motives, emotions, and thoughts. Each of these touches on who one is and can contribute to one's growth and to conversion. The process of conversion is a lifetime endeavor and is never achieved alone but only with the help of the community and God's grace.

Nature and Grace

In spite of sin and its deceptive influence on the human mind and psyche, the power of good, truth, and beauty can triumph. The presence of Christ through the Spirit is grace, a power stronger than the forces of evil. John Paul II says, "Grace, in cooperation with human freedom, constitutes that mysterious presence of God in history which is Providence" (*Centesimus Annus* 59) Sin did not have the final word on Calvary because the resurrected Word was spoken in the risen Jesus. By virtue of the resurrection, all of life is immersed in grace and is present in the sacrament of the church. Grace elicits from us what is most human and can bring each person to the fullness of humanity.

At various periods in the church's history, redemption was limited to redemption of the soul. The body was not considered redeemed and was seen as the source of evil and a vehicle for sin. Heresies such as Manichaeism, Stoicism, and Jansenism maintained that what pertained to the body, the physical and emotional, was animal-like and not truly human. "Animal drives," such as physical needs or strong emotions, demeaned the human being and were unworthy of a person. Not agreeing with these views, the church strove to establish a balanced view of the human body by declaring such beliefs heretical. However, these perceptions of humanity tainted popular and religious views of sexuality, relationships in marriage, and interpersonal communication for centuries. This was seen in sexual morality that too readily judged sexual pleasure in marriage as lust. Because of these misconstrued perceptions of the human body, a dualism of body and soul emerged in philosophy as well as in theology, especially during the Enlightenment.

Because of the triumph of grace in the resurrection, the old dualism of body and soul cannot be used to argue for the evil of the human body. Rather, nature is seen as redeemed, as having the opportunity and invitation to walk in the fullness of life with God. Indeed, through redemption we can come to realize our humanity more fully.

Grace is given freely. A relationship with Jesus is never forced but stands as an invitation that can be accepted or rejected. Like other relationships, the one with Jesus must be marked with desire, active participation, and responsibility. Passivity before the invitation of God would imply that God has responsibility for our salvation and we have none. That lopsided kind of relationship is dehumanizing and signifies a lack of mutuality. True humanness is achieved when there is involvement, even struggle and discipline, to achieve a goal, especially in the moral life. Like a tug of war between what is most human and what is humanly degrading, this struggle continues in the birth of each new infant. Every person feels the tension between goodness and evil. Evil — disguised as good, a false reservoir from which we can fulfill our needs — ever parades itself in the most attractive mien. We are often duped by its allurement. While money, position, influence, power, and possessions are good in themselves, we are daily enticed by these as the sure means to human fulfillment and happiness. Without grace in the form of inspiration, moral support, and strong admonitions provided by moral norms and church leaders, most of us would succumb more frequently to the false enticements of evil.

As a redeemed people, sin no longer has the power to define us. Our humanity has been raised beyond the confines of sin through the life, death, and resurrection of Jesus. He has ended the hold of sin over humanity. In the person of Jesus we have a model for moral living and a reason for hope as we continue the struggle of good over evil.

Person-Centered Morality

Person-centered morality is based on the social and relational nature of a human being. Communication is a necessity for all social and relational interactions. A person-centered morality would therefore include communication and dialogue as key components.

Social Beings

> The moral life is influenced more by significant persons in our lives and how closely we identify with them than it is influenced by explicit moral instruction.
>
> — RICHARD GULA, *Reason Informed by Faith*

Communication is the condition for learning. Without the ability to receive communication through hearing and eyesight, the learner is severely handicapped. Modeling behavior by a significant person is the primary means of learning morality. In comparison, textbooks are limited contributors to anyone's moral development. Significant persons are those who love us, inspire and encourage us, care for us, and lead us. These people most often are parents, spouses, grandparents, teachers, religious, neighbors, friends, and leaders.

Relationships are key to moral learning. The love of one person can touch the heart of another and open doors to learning that previously were closed. Recall the teacher who most inspired you to learn, or recall an influential person in your life. That person most often is one who loved and encouraged you, who was wise and was there when you were in need. Because of his or her love and interest, your self-confidence rose and you could embrace new vistas of learning and achievement. Clearly the dynamism of one person's life has power to effect change in another person's life. This same reality touches one's moral life. From the significant "love people" in early childhood we learn what is morally right and wrong. Although early judgments of childhood are based on wanting to please our "love people," the moral lessons become patterns and then habits of moral living. In adulthood we can appropriate those early learnings and make them truly our own by moral decisions employing adult freedom.

Moral learning occurs in relationships because human beings are social beings. At Vatican II, the Council Fathers recognized the social and communal nature of people when they stated: "For by his innermost nature man is a social being, and unless he relates himself to others he can neither live nor develop his potential" (*Gaudium et Spes* 12).

The Community

Moral values, traditions, and norms are relayed not just through individual persons but also through communities of belief. This is demonstrated through the diversity of moral stands taken by communities of faith. Some, like the Quakers, are strongly opposed to war while some branches of the Islamic and Jewish religions support "holy wars" based on religious convictions. Some religious communities, like the Roman Catholic Church, are opposed to abortion and artificial means of birth control while most Protestant denominations believe such decisions ought to be made in the personal domain. Whatever the moral stand of a faith community, that stand is difficult to maintain by individuals without the support of the community.

Person-centered morality includes community-centered morality. Irish moralist Enda McDonagh rightly states that "the Word or self-giving of God to mankind forms mankind into a community.... The true response of man to God's gift is the promotion of the community of mankind, the development of mankind as God's people."[7] In community, moral wisdom can be passed on from the forerunners in the faith whose wisdom has stood the test of time. Some giants in the faith have endured persecution and martyrdom even in this day. Learning the moral life in a community setting enables younger members to see the moral attitudes, stances, convictions, and actions modeled by older members of the community. The strong love and courage of some members have been recognized by the community who assisted in their canonization as saints. The lives of saints stand as vibrant witnesses because their very lives tell us about discipleship and moral living. The moral "textbook" of a well-lived life is far superior to any moral lecture or well-penned book. People learn about the moral life chiefly from each other, the methodology used by Jesus. All other means of learning are merely supplements and help us reflect on experiences gained through interactions with people and events.

The Effects of Human Nature on Our Acts

> Acts in God's eye what in God's eye he is —
> Christ. For Christ plays in ten thousand places,
> Lovely in limbs, and lovely in eyes not his
> To the Father through the features of men's faces.
>
> — GERARD MANLEY HOPKINS,
> "As Kingfishers Catch Fire"

A person-centered morality focuses on communication and learning, relationships and community. The primary person to consider is Jesus, whose human acts are extended through our own. Obviously, human acts have widespread effects on our lives. It is important then to consider human acts in the light of the person performing them. The concrete circumstances of a person's life help determine an act as morally right or wrong, as seriously or less seriously evil. In the past, moral theology analyzed moral acts apart from the person performing them. Manuals for confessors and textbooks of moral theology presented clear cases and norms that delineated, even dissected, a human act into all its component parts: before the act (intention), the act itself, and after the act (consequences). Because of this generalized and noncontextual way of dealing with moral acts, a legalized morality emerged. Problems developed under this approach to morality, one being that holiness and conversion were interpreted as obedience to the letter of the law rather than conversion of heart and mind. However, merely doing right actions did not touch the heart, which is the source of good and evil, and it did not help church members to address relational, emotional, and attitudinal areas of morality.

It was necessary with the revisions of Vatican II to examine the nature of human acts in terms of conversion, discipleship, and redemption. With a Christocentric theology, morality examines the approach of Jesus when he confronted immoral acts. For Jesus, an act never stood in isolation but rather stood against the backdrop of family, relationships, job, responsibilities, education, and roles. Jesus dealt with the person as an individual within her or his context: the woman caught in adultery, Matthew the tax collector, the man born blind and his parents, the Samaritan woman, the man possessed by demons, and even Jesus' apostle, Judas. Jesus also considered the structures of evil within their context: the hypocrisy of the Pharisees, misuse of the temple by merchants, heavy taxes by the Romans, the weakness of magistrates like Pilate. By taking into account the circumstances and context of moral acts, Jesus showed the importance of reason that discriminates between the various factors affecting a decision.

Reason and Will

> This objectivity-truth is achieved, on the one hand, through right understanding of the revealed word of God, insofar as it contains morally significant affirmations, on the other hand, through the right moral understanding of man's concrete reality, in which connection, obviously, the light of revelation and the moral understanding of man are not to be viewed as two completely unrelated possibilities.
>
> —JOSEPH FUCHS, S.J., "The Absoluteness of Moral Terms"

Fundamental to any understanding of human nature and persons are reason and will. We human beings have the capacity to use intellectual gifts of reason and will to govern our lives. We are responsible for the development and use of reason and will, but at the same time these gifts afford us tremendous freedom for creativity, happiness, and fulfillment. Through the use of reason, we can discover in human nature and in creation the "reasonable" thing to do. But "reasonable," applied to moral theology, cannot be misconstrued as "practical," "using common sense," or some middle ground of moral compromise. Reason means *recta ratio,* right reason, which involves evaluative observation, understanding, and judgment based on cognitive or intuitive perception. Right reason, according to Josef Fuchs, means right understanding of the Word of God and of what is right for human beings. The moral law is inscribed as right reason in the "nature" of human beings, or, as St. Paul says, the moral law is "engraved on the heart" (Rom. 2:15).[8]

We reason rightly when the final goal of life, union with God, motivates us to act in a certain way. With such motivation, morally good acts will be chosen, even when there may be difficulty and pain. At times reason may seem "unreasonable," as in the case of people who are jailed because they uphold higher moral values than the civil law inscribes, couples who endure tremendous hardships in caring for a handicapped child or spouse, men or women who quit a job because they would have to compromise moral values.

•

A human being is the congresswoman facing a tough decision about voting for a bill that contains facets contrary to her moral beliefs but that has financial benefits and programs for the needy people of her district.

Doing the reasonable thing is sometimes difficult to discern, as in the case of the congresswoman whose decisions bear mixed consequences. What is the reasonable and morally right decision that is not merely utilitarian?

Again, "reasonable" is not always synonymous with "reason" — some will go "the extra mile" that seems beyond reason because their faith tells them this is the most reasonable thing to do. Conflicts between "reasonable" and "reason" arise when one tries to accomplish a moral good. Today families and members of the medical profession agonize over what amount of care for a seriously ill, or even a terminal, patient is within reason. The levels of nutrition, hydration, surgical procedures, and hospitalization are but a few of the moral questions confronting a family and physician who want to do all that can reasonably be done for a dear one and patient.

In the face of moral dilemmas, moralists developed a system called casuistry, which guided the clergy in determining the "reasonable" thing to do for specific situations. Casuistry studied and evaluated a "case" in terms of moral norms. As long as the "case" was taken in the abstract without the human factors of circumstances and context involved, the casuistic system was and still is valuable. However, casuistry often fell short of the complex demands of contemporary society and its moral questions.[9]

In addition to reason, human will plays a fundamental role in determining the human act. Each of us wants to be happy and live a peaceful life. At times we do not have the "will" to choose those things that would make us happy and live in peace. A woman wants to lose twenty-five pounds but does not have the willpower to forgo chocolate cake and cream in her coffee. A young man wants to be on the varsity basketball squad but is unwilling to practice the many hours such a position would demand. Will means more than "want"; will refers to the inner commitment and discipline of the self to a certain line of thinking and action. It involves motivation, desire, and the energy to bring the desired results into reality. Will is significant in moral reasoning because it determines the amount of personal involvement one has in a given issue. The thief who schemes and connives for months about abducting funds from his business partner is vastly more involved morally than the woman who impulsively shoplifts a toy rattle for her baby boy.

An act is human when it involves the person and engages human reason and will. Insofar as the act is freely and reflectively chosen and intends good, it mirrors true humanity: the best self. It can then be called a truly human act. If the act is done impulsively, is forced, or is done with no reflection about the act or its consequences, it can be said to be less "human." Implicit in this understanding of human acts is an understanding of the human being as one whose life is oriented to ultimate values and who maintains a harmonious balance of all aspects of the self: personality, intellect, physical drives, will, and emotions. Such a balance is difficult to achieve, but with the model of Jesus' own life to motivate us, with grace, and with the support of a Christian community, Christians can strive to live the most human life possible.

Conclusion

Disciples of Jesus are called to full humanity. To be fully human means to be true to all that makes a person human and is shared with other human beings, but it also means to be true to what makes us uniquely ourselves. Who we are in personality, character, gender, and life-calling is unique. We are created by God to be human and to share that humanity with others, but we are also created uniquely ourselves. The dignity of persons is based on creation by God. Our response to God is to be true to who we are as creatures of God. This is one basic axiom of moral theology.

Our desires reveal our desire for God. The desires for truth, love, beauty, and justice are present in the human breast and carry us beyond the satisfaction of human relationships and the pleasures of this world. Our desires transcend our ability to fulfill them in this life because we are made in the image of God who alone fills our desires. Our needs also reveal who we are. Social needs reveal the importance of people and relationships. Without them we neither grow nor reach any degree of satisfaction and happiness.

A person-centered morality gives adequate consideration to us as human beings, to God's presence in our lives, and to a hope for redemption and triumph over the power of evil. Human acts can be addressed in the context of our humanity and redemption. With a balance of these factors we can arrive at moral judgments that are adequate for the human person.

Notes

1. John W. Donohue, S.J., "Of Many Things," *America* 172, no. 2 (January 28, 1995): 2.

2. See ibid.

3. Timothy E. O'Connell, *Principles for a Catholic Morality* (New York: Harper and Row, 1990), 68.

4. Psychologists study the conscious and unconscious dimensions of the human psyche. Much knowledge of the self is hidden in the human unconscious, which through psychoanalysis can be made conscious to a certain extent.

5. Karl Rahner, *Foundations of Christian Faith* (New York: Crossroad, 1978), 46.

6. David Tracy, *Blessed Rage for Order* (New York: Seabury, 1979), 108–9.

7. Enda McDonagh, *Invitation and Response: Essays in Christian Moral Theology* (New York: Sheed and Ward, 1972), 53.

8. Joseph Fuchs, "The Absoluteness of Moral Terms," in *Readings in Moral Theology,* ed. Charles E. Curran and Richard A. McCormick (New York: Paulist Press, 1979), 1:110.

9. See James Keenan and Thomas Shannon, *The Context of Casuistry* (Washington, D.C.: Georgetown University Press, 1995); and Albert R. Jonsen, *The Abuse of Casuistry* (Berkeley: University of California Press, 1988).

Chapter 5

THE REALITY OF EVIL AND SIN

Nick made an appointment with his new boss to discuss the problems he and his construction workers were having with the inferior building materials they were receiving. "We're overcharging our customers for these materials that won't last more than two years," he said. As expected, his boss fired Nick for being unable to adjust to the new management and not "getting with the program." Fifty years old and out of work, still paying off a house and two kids' college educations — Nick had to deal with one face of evil.

Evil wears many faces. Sometimes it comes in the form of pain and stress such as Nick felt when he went home and told his wife the bad news. Nick experienced moral evil at his job — the moral evil we call sin, which here was characterized by deviousness and deliberate harm done to another. Moral evils are chosen and involve personal deliberation. Evil can take nonmoral forms such as natural disasters, physical illness, or accidents that are not intended or chosen and that are beyond human control. This chapter will explore the realities of evil, particularly moral evil or sin.

The Contemporary Face of Evil

The contemporary face of evil has the look of starving children in Africa and South America; it has the desperate look of men and women trying to find work in order to support themselves and their children; it has the look of well-heeled executives whose only interest is financial gain; evil shows its face in political "bargaining" that gives people personal power. Contemporary evil is present in the political decisions that keep some countries dependent on others while other countries prosper economically. Refugees and immigrants show the world the face of evil created by oppressive regimes and desolate poverty. The buying and selling of illegal drugs is another contemporary sign of moral evil. However, drug abuse by a young man doing a dance in the middle of a busy highway at 8:30 A.M. because he is high on drugs or by an addict slouched in a doorway may constitute only nonmoral evil: these men may lack personal freedom to make choices for the good. Marriages that end in screaming and brutality, hatred and violence, remind us that moral evil is harbored within the walls of homes, not just on the streets. Contemporary society reveals the visages of evil in many forms: social ills; deterioration of interpersonal relationships; economic and political systems that favor the powerful and sacrifice the powerless; structures of evil in offices of police, education, social welfare, law, medicine, and even religion. While much of the moral evil described above is structural in nature and is social sin, there is also evil that originates from individual persons, which is called personal sin.

The Reality of Sin

Network newscasts are often updates on sin in the contemporary world. As demonstrated above, the power of evil is present in the acts of individual persons and in systemic ways through structures of evil. Sin is real when love is absent, when power and domination are the primary motivations for actions, when pride rules decisions of conscience, when relationships are reduced to sexual satisfaction, when injustice succeeds and persons are devalued.

One could examine the innumerable manifestations of sin in contemporary society and miss the core reality of sin: *at root, sin is spiritual in nature and reflects the lack of a personal relationship of love with God, self, and others.* Sin denies the reality of God who is goodness, truth, and love and sets up another reality opposed to the existence of God. Basically sin erects strange gods: power, pride, injustice, passions. The first commandment, "You shall have no strange gods before me," encompasses all of the Ten Commandments because it requires a relationship of faith in the one God and gives primacy of place to God. When the relationship with God is weak, then sin is an easy choice and we erect "strange gods." While power and economic strength are neither good nor bad, the "strange gods" of First World countries are too often cloaked in power and dominance, built with the "gold and silver" of individuals whose primary value is selfish gain, self-serving power, and position. Richard M. Gula describes sin as the "arrogance of power": "The covenant says that we are already established as persons of worth by the gratuitous love of God, nothing else. But . . . the heart sets out to secure its loveableness by its own striving. The arrogance of power is the imperial 'I' living as though it must make itself great."[1]

Another moral theologian, Karl H. Peschke, assesses the morality of actions in terms of love.[2] The supreme commandment is to "love God above all things and our neighbor as ourselves." From this commandment all other commandments and moral norms are derived, and from this commandment of love all judgments of good and evil can be made. The first three commandments pertain to love of God while the remaining seven indicate ways of loving others and oneself. Actions that offend against the norm of love are sinful. Actions that express and support love are virtues.

Theologians working with the poor to attain liberation from poverty are called liberation theologians. These theologians think injustice and inequality among people are the prime expressions of sin.[3] Human dignity and justice are disregarded by the very structures that are to ensure these Christian values. Eighty percent of the weapons in the world are owned by nations on the UN's Security Council. The United States is one of the main suppliers of weapons to the world market. The U.S. Catholic bishops have expressed their concern about the sale of military weapons:

> The bishops accused the United States Government of aggressively supporting arms sales through military aid and other means as a way of helping the United States arms industry at a time of decreasing defense spending. The United States now supplies half the world's arms exports and provides more than 70 percent of the arms going to the third world. In 1994 United States Government military aid and sales amounted to $12.5 billion, while direct sales by United States companies amounted to an additional $25.6 billion.[4]

While efforts are made to better the conditions of poor nations, First World countries gain economically through the sale of weapons to Third World countries, sales that do not better the living conditions of the people. The injustices and inequality of peoples are evident in human rights violations in some poor countries where individuals have simply "disappeared" because they opposed the injustices against their people.

Individual acts and structures of sin are manifest in many ways, but the arrogance of power, the absence of love, and injustice seem to be prevalent patterns of sin today. Each age and each culture has predominant patterns of sin unique to it. When a person makes choices for evil, the individual acts can lead to patterns of behavior and patterns of attitudes and values that become part of a person's moral arena.

The Fundamental Option

Patterns of evil produce a way of life that is reinforced with each act and choice for evil. A person who lives this way finally makes a decision or fundamental option for evil rather than good.[5] The fundamental option for evil is a gradual move consisting of individual acts that pave the way for a final decision, one that can always be reversed because of God's grace and faithful love. The Congregation for the Doctrine of the Faith issued a document on sexual ethics, *Persona Humana,* in 1975 that explains the relationship between mortal sin and the theory of the fundamental option:

> In reality, it is precisely the fundamental option which in the last resort defines a person's moral disposition. But it can be completely changed by particular acts, especially when, as often happens, these have been prepared for by previous more superficial acts. Whatever the case, it is wrong to say that particular acts are not enough to constitute mortal sin.

The fundamental option for evil demonstrates the radical nature of sin. *In its full meaning, sin is a fundamental choice for evil, a basic rejection of God and love in one's life and the erection of a false god.* By replacing the living God with a false god, one rejects the spiritual dimension, and that rejection changes one's entire attitude toward all of material creation, including oneself.

It is difficult to conceive of someone choosing evil as a way of life until one encounters such a person. Many years ago, in doing hospital visitations, I entered the room of an elderly man whom I will call Sam. When I entered his room, Sam was seated in a chair by his bed. Sam greeted me with a cold and hostile stare that was his only form of communication during the entire time I was in his room. Since he appeared to be so noncommunicative and distant, I inquired about him and later read information from the newspapers about him and his family. I learned Sam was the "Godfather" of the Mafia organization in a nearby city. Two of his sons had become notorious because of their crimes and their imprisonment for numerous charges including murder. Sam headed the Mafia for many years but was never convicted for his involvements. Obviously, his sons were given the reins of leadership from their father, who probably taught them how to bend the civil and moral law according to their liking. Money, power, violence, and wrongdoing became the "strange gods" that took over the life of this Mafia-centered family. This way of life did not emerge from one single act but was learned over a period of time.

While I was doing hospital chaplaincy work, the nine-year-old son of a Southside Chicago man was brought into the hospital and transferred to the neurosurgical unit where I was working. The boy had been beaten on the head with a bat and was in a coma. Police detectives believed someone had meant to kill the boy after he had witnessed the rape and murder of his teenage sister in the early morning hours. The detective in charge of the case suspected the father and was eager to be present when the boy awoke so he could observe the boy's reactions to his father. He was certain the father was guilty because he said little and was "as cool as a cucumber." In fact, the father was extremely worried and in great distress. Within a few weeks, the investigators found they had wrongly suspected the father and found the killer, a young man who lived across the street, a man who had known the girl for a long time. Early in the morning of the attack, the father had left the home to take his wife to the emergency room, something observed by the young man who had entered the house and attempted to seduce the girl. The crimes were witnessed by the nine-year-old brother, whom the young man also tried to kill. These crimes of rape and murder did not occur suddenly but had precursors in the thoughts and imaginings of the young man, which led to intentions of evil and finally to violence and murder. While these are serious objective evils, sadly, the young man lived in an environment where murders and violence were almost daily occurrences. This environment could easily have tainted the young man's subjective culpability and freedom regarding his objectively immoral acts. A fundamental option implies freedom to choose good or evil and a correctly formed conscience that guides moral thinking. A fundamental option for evil is carved by small acts that finally lead to the larger consent to the way of evil. This is sin in the stark sense: a rejection of God and God's love through a choice for evil expressed in individual acts. Such sin is personal sin because of the full personal involvement of an individual.

Moral and Nonmoral Evil

We have examined many aspects of moral evil, but the dimensions of nonmoral evil affect each of us. Some examples can help us differentiate between the evil we fully intend and the evil that regrettably happens through no intention or choice on our part.

The hardest admission for most people to make is, "It was my fault." That short sentence is difficult because it acknowledges human limitation and failure. We like to succeed, not fail. Most of us want to be praised and accepted as likable people. We do not want to "lose face" and suffer embarrassment for our mistakes and failures. Humiliation and rejection are painful. In acknowledging fault we may have to admit our guilt as well. Maybe there was no personal fault because the best effort was given, but it was not enough. Perhaps there was fault because no effort was made. "It was my fault" is then difficult to admit.

Bill was drunk and driving and killed nine-year-old Kurt, who was riding his bike home from school. Harry loved the casinos, so it was not surprising that half of his paycheck was lost at the gaming tables the weekend after pay day; he was the only source of income for a wife and two children. Ellen had a violent temper that erupted when her two-year-old got into the cupboards for the third time one morning. She struck her daughter, who became unconscious when she fell against a table. Bill, Harry, and Ellen had to admit "It was my fault." Were the actions of Bill, Harry, and Ellen moral evils?

For the acts of Bill, Harry, and Ellen to be moral evils, they must have intended to do evil, must have permitted or provided circumstances for evil to occur, and must have attempted to carry out the evil intended. When these elements of sin are missing, we cannot place moral fault on the person, but we can see nonmoral evil present. Bill, Harry, and Ellen did not intend or foresee evil, but the evil consequences of their actions could have been prevented, with help. Moral decisions or actions that lack freedom or knowledge of the evil are not culpable moral evils. Personality patterns of temper and addictions to alcohol and gambling rob people of freedom so they are prone to act in compulsive and addictive ways. With help they are able to manage these problem situations. When one has some ability to control choices, consequences, and circumstances of an action, then one is responsible for that action. One is culpable for a moral action to the degree one is responsible. Certainly, each person must do all possible to become knowledgeable and free in terms of addictive behaviors, emotional control, or other patterns that may generate negative consequences. The actions of Bill, Harry, and Ellen can be nonmoral evil or have lessened culpability depending on each one's level of freedom and responsibility in the situation.

In all of these cases there is a mixture of personal fault and human limitations with no direct intention to do evil. Nevertheless, as human beings we must admit our personal deficiencies and accept responsibility for the wrong and pain we intentionally cause; when there are unforeseen consequences to our actions, in justice we must do all we can to right the situation and alleviate the pain we caused. Admission of our fault is crucial for retribution and justice to be done to those who have suffered, but admission of fault can also greatly help the one who caused the harm. Maturity and growth in responsibility, self-knowledge, and care for others can be gained. However, the "overguilty" person may claim total fault when that is not the case. This might indicate there are psychological problems related to scrupulosity. On a theological level, the true admission is that we are human and unable to do and see and know all that affects a situation.

The church teaches that some acts are always morally wrong regardless of a person's intention or the circumstances that led to the evil act. This is true of acts such as genocide, murder, rape, and incest. These acts are called moral absolutes and are considered sins and reprehensible crimes that no excuse, mitigating circumstances, or intention of the actor can justify — even when the actor believes the evil act will bring about good at some level. This false sense of mission cannot justify the immoral act.[6] In less serious situations, more discernment is required to make a moral judgment. When no evil is intended and the best efforts and judgments have been made, given the knowledge available, it could be said that no intentional moral evil occurred. Moral theologians distinguish between the evil that is intended, which is moral evil or sin, and unintended evil, which occurs from accidents, disasters of nature, and quirks of chance. These are nonmoral evils, sometimes called physical (or "ontic") evils.[7] The forest fires in the Rocky Mountains have claimed the lives of experienced firefighters and destroyed hundreds of homes; the Mississippi River flooded the plains of the Midwest; a collision of a train and a stalled car caused death: these are classified as nonmoral evil because no moral wrong was intended, and the evil that occurred could not have been foreseen or even prevented. Forces greater than human power were in control.

Moral evil is not accidental and does not happen by chance or as a natural disaster; rather it happens because it is planned and intended. Although many would like to blame someone else for moral evil ("The devil made me do it!"), it is actually the choice of human beings that causes sin or moral evil.

The Person: Sinful and Redeemed

Individual desires that reflect our dark side, our sinful nature, can manifest our social nature in the form of social ills. People caused the devastation of World War I, World War II, and the Vietnam War. These wars involved atrocities to whole nations, murder of ethnic groups, devastation of the infrastructures of countries, and the consequent evils of poverty, starvation, and disease. Innocent people were killed and left homeless. The spirit of entire societies was all but destroyed in each war. Even today injustices abound in the court systems of the world; we see the disparity between the "haves" and the "have nots," crime and violence, famine and poverty. These evils can be traced to the "boundless desires" of human beings.

Moral theology examines the range of desires that emerges from the human being. Both the good and the evil desires signify something about us and express our relationship to all of reality: to ourselves, to others, and to God.

Pope John Paul II places the human person at the center of moral thinking and moral decisions. How can the pope place such emphasis on sinful, imperfect, and flawed human beings? He cannot reasonably do that unless he balances a person-centered perspective with a grace perspective that sees human beings as redeemed. Persons are sinful *and* redeemed. Adam and Eve disobeyed God and chose to be equal to God in knowledge, and we have shared their predisposition for pride and disobedience to moral injunctions. We seek positions of power and prestige, envy those who have more, speak and act out of prejudice, seek our own pleasure, and often show little respect for those with less. Loose sexual mores and marriage statistics demonstrate our inability to remain committed.

We sin as individuals, and there is ample evidence that peoples — groups — can be collectively sinful. World War I and World War II demonstrated the abilities of many peoples to kill and hurt each other. Sophisticated weaponry, nuclear weapons, and millions of lives were used to destroy the enemy, but "the enemy is us." Unable to learn from these devastating wars, countries went on to other wars: the Korean War, the Vietnam War, ethnic and tribal wars, and guerrilla warfare that to this day harms and destroys peoples. We have only to look at the extensive drug trafficking and the inequalities among peoples to know that sin has not been limited to individuals but is embedded in social structures of governments and nations. The educational, health-care, social-service, and military systems of the United States are but a few of the social structures that are enmeshed in patterns of sin. These sins found in the structures of society are called social sin. The social sin of these structures is fed by the arrogance of power, described by Richard Gula:

> The arrogance of power is the imperial "I" living as though it must make itself great.... Sin as the arrogant use of power separates us from life-giving and loving relationships.... Self-serving interests destroy bonds of peace and justice, and spread conditions of fear, hatred, and violence which usher in the disharmony of the world which we know as social sin — the co-operation in the continued maintenance of oppressive structures of society.[8]

John Paul II was aware of social sin and of the sinfulness of human nature when he suggested that we recall our sins as a community of Christian believers for the past two thousand years. Only with a look to our past can we constructively live in the new millennium.

Systemic and Structural Evil

Evil exists even when great efforts are made to prevent it. Ethnic wars in the former Soviet Union are forms of moral and nonmoral evil playing themselves out in the daily news. Some of the wars are intended to destroy, harm, and kill because of prejudice and revenge. This is moral evil. However, not all the consequences are fully intended: innocent people are killed; the infrastructures of the country are reduced to rubble; people are homeless; disease and famine plague warring tribes and nations. These effects are the result of moral evil.

The structures of sin present in these situations are systemic and continue to effect evil for people and the environment. *Structures of sin* are those patterns that become modes of operation within institutions such as government and finance; these structures can become so extensive that they permeate the entire system. Systemic evil can be found throughout an entire system. An example of structures of sin and systemic evil can be found in the problems facing UN peacekeepers in parts of Africa. There seem to be no viable means, despite the efforts of UN peacekeeping forces and international efforts, to provide humanitarian aid in the form of food, shelter, clothing, and medical help to some areas. Millions of dollars and thousands of personnel have tried to alleviate the problems confronting Africans.

Still Africa faces dire hunger, poverty, disease, and tribal wars that destroy families, tribes, and countries because the structures of government, economy, education, and political systems are ineffective. Many analysts believe corruption (or immorality) is partly to blame for the problems. Recent statistics show 71 percent of the people in the world with AIDS are African. This means 1.7 million people in Africa suffer from the disease. Other diseases that are treated in First and Second World countries are not treated in Third World countries because of poverty, fighting, and lack of medical care. These evils are structured and systemic in nature.

To change the conditions strapping Africa and Third World countries would require mammoth efforts. What is needed is an overthrow of the entire system that causes evil. This would require a reordering of entire social and political systems, as well as the environmental and economic structures of countries. "Naysayers" take a pessimistic attitude, believing change is impossible to achieve. "Why pour more money and supplies into a hopeless situation?" "Let them take care of themselves. After all, they are doing this to themselves." These assumptions breed an isolationist attitude contrary to Christian belief in ties that bind together all the peoples of the earth.

Types of Sin

Sin is the choice of evil rather than good. Using freedom and the ability to choose, people can decide what they want and desire. Ideally they are attracted to the good, to truth, to love, and to justice and will want to choose those in the many ways they are present in ordinary life. Sin, however, is the choice to follow what is not good, to choose lies over truth, lack of charity over love, and injustice rather than justice. Within the area of sin there is a spectrum of seriousness or intention, matter, and willingness to comply with evil. Categorizing by "types of sin" takes account of this spectrum. We will here examine two basic types of sin: (1) actual sin and (2) original sin. Actual sin can be subdivided into the categories of mortal sin, venial sin, and social sin.

Actual Sin

Actual sins are the concrete acts we as human beings commit in contradiction of God's love.[9] Depending upon the personal investment of the person, the act constitutes either a mortal sin or a venial sin.

The church's tradition uses three criteria to determine that a sin is mortal: (1) serious moral matter; (2) sufficient reflection and clear knowledge of the immoral matter; and (3) full consent of the will — the free choice to commit moral wrong. When all three criteria are met and there is a full surrender to a way of life that is evil, then the act at issue and state of life spell death to a relationship with God, which is why the term "mortal" is used. Never, however, is God's love withdrawn, for like the father of the Prodigal Son, God always lovingly welcomes one who has strayed.

Venial sin lacks one of the elements given by the tradition. There may be less serious moral matter, some lack of knowledge about the moral wrong, or some lack of freedom in choosing sin. Venial sin is often called "sin by analogy" because it is only like, or analogous to, the full sense of sin; it is unlike mortal sin because it is not the complete rejection of God.

It is a mistake to treat venial sin as a minimal infraction of a moral law. If we view venial sin as something minor, unimportant, and even negligible, it takes on greater power. Small acts of moral wrong gradually erode the desire for good, truth, love, and justice. Almost imperceptibly they dull the moral senses to the mind and heart of Christ. This can be compared to eleven-year-old Steve, who became upset while he and his friends watched a movie portraying graphic violence. His friends enjoyed the movie and laughed loudly at many of the most cruel and vicious scenes. Gradually Steve learned to tolerate the violence and could watch movies of this type with his friends. Violence, murder, torture, and harm eventually did not seem unreal but a way of being. Recent studies show the high correlation between violence on the screen and acts of violence by juvenile offenders who watch this type of film. Because young people are less able to distinguish between fictional and real-life situations, there is a merging of the two into a warped sense of what is moral and acceptable. They become morally numb to the value and worth of human life. Just so, repeated acts of venial sin numb the person to moral values.

There is another type of actual sin called social sin. This sin became more clearly defined through the Vatican II document *Gaudium et Spes*. Here the Council Fathers draw connections between social structures and personal sin:

> To be sure the disturbances which so frequently occur in the social order result in part from the natural tensions of economic,

political, and social forms. But at a deeper level they flow from man's pride and selfishness, which contaminate even the social sphere. When the structure of affairs is flawed by the consequences of sin, man, already born with a bent toward evil, finds there the new inducements to sin, which cannot be overcome without strenuous efforts and the assistance of grace. (*Gaudium et Spes* 25)

Popes after Vatican II were aware of the social dimensions of sin. They addressed issues of political oppression, poverty, violence, economic injustice, prejudice, military systems, and even the social sins of the church. Pope John Paul II speaks of social sin in *Reconciliatio et Penitentia* (1984). He shows the connection between personal acts and social systems that are sinful. He says of social sin:

It is a case of the very personal sins of those who cause or support evil or who exploit it; of those who are in a position to avoid, eliminate or at least limit certain social evils but who fail to do so out of laziness, fear or the conspiracy of silence, through secret complicity or indifference; of those who take refuge in the supposed impossibility of changing the world and also of those who sidestep the effort and sacrifice required, producing specious reasons of a higher order. (16)

It is clear the pope believes efforts must be made to change immoral social structures. The pope is very aware that some acts, structures, and systems have far-reaching social implications that affect large bodies of people. They create webs that bind people and make it almost impossible to be free from the situation.

The "cycle of poverty," which affects many African-Americans, Hispanics, and other minority groups in the United States, is one example of social sin. The housing projects of large cities are shameful testimony of social systems and structures that keep some people in poverty because of their race. They do not receive the same opportunities for education that other citizens enjoy because inner-city schools tend to have inadequate supplies, poorly equipped and maintained buildings, lower standards, and more students per teacher. The poor are unable to move out of the inner city because their poor education does not prepare them for the job market or for more than minimum-wage jobs. Without good jobs there is little income, so families become dependent on the government to provide for them. The government frequently puts little into supplying adequate housing to those who are unemployed because of pressure from taxpayers to stop supporting those who are "unwilling" to work. And so the cycle of poverty goes on to create what has recently been called the Fourth World.

In his encyclical *Sollicitudo Rei Socialis,* Pope John Paul II speaks of the Fourth World, a term that is "used not for the so-called less advanced countries, but also and especially for the bands of great or extreme poverty in countries of medium and high income" (14, n. 31). "Inner-city blight," "housing projects," or "core" are all terms that evoke a picture of the Fourth World within First World countries like the United States. The presence of such large economic discrepancies between peoples in the same country speaks of social sin.

Often related to economic inequities is institutionalized prejudice, another form of social sin. Prejudice is based on some factor that distinguishes one person from another. Most often the basis for prejudice is power, money, color of skin, gender (prejudice being most frequently directed toward women), age (especially as applied to older citizens), ethnic group, sexual orientation (especially pertaining to the homosexual population and persons with AIDS), and place of origin. The structures that perpetuate the social sin of prejudice are often bound to economic structures, politics, legal systems, educational and social-welfare institutions, and law enforcement. The minority group is in a powerless position. Because one group of people is benefiting from the prejudicial and flawed structures, other structures under their control are also made to serve the interests of that ruling group. It is extremely difficult to undo these interconnected structures because they are so enmeshed in the businesses and personal lives of the advantaged. As a result, the economic gaps between the rich and the poor grow daily:

> The gap between the richest and the poorest in the United States has reached its widest point in forty years and is greater than in most industrialized countries. In 1987, the wealthiest 40 percent of American families received 67.8 percent of the national family income, while the poorest 40 percent of families received 15.4 percent. The growth of income inequality is particularly stark, given the varying rates of income growth among different family types. The income of the average family in the lowest two quintiles of the income distribution fell $741 between 1978 and 1987, while the income of the average family in the upper

two quintiles rose $3,031. The income of the typical family in
the top 10 percent rose $8,119 during this period.[10]

The structures of inequality are maintained and supported by human
beings who are unwilling to change them. That is social sin.

Social sin exists in the intention, will, and actions of human
beings. This view is contrary to those who argue institutions are
impersonal, objective realities. They believe institutions are impossible to change because they are inhuman and too large and complex
to be controlled by people. They do not believe people create and
control institutions. As a consequence, their passive belief condones
social sin and suggests helpless compliance to its power. The disciple
of Jesus takes a contrary view and challenges this outlook, believing
human beings can change and control what human beings created.
Baptism affirms this, affirms that the power of evil, even when manifested as widespread social sin, is not the final power or the ruling
power over human beings.[11]

Original Sin

The pervasiveness of sin in the world is due not just to actual sin —
from the beginning of humanity, sin entered the world as original
sin. More than an act, "Original sin is the theological code word for
the human condition of living in a world where we are influenced by
more evil than what we do ourselves."[12] Because of the environment
in which people are born and raised, they experience patterns, structures, and acts of sin. Some would say original sin is due to the sin of
Adam and Eve, while others believe the origins of sin were intrinsic
to the human species. The proclivity to sin rather than obedience and
love is part of human nature and the human environment. As noted
above, the Council Fathers spoke of the influence of original sin in
Gaudium et Spes.

The church does not believe that original sin determines humanity
as sinful. Rather, the sacrament of Baptism determines the triumph
of good over sin, the power of resurrection and new life over the
power of spiritual death in sin. Baptism brings the person into full
union with Christ and the church by washing away original sin.
Should the baptism be that of an infant, the little one can begin life
with open love and total acceptance and union with God, thanks to
the power of the sacrament. From the first days of life, sin does not
have power to determine the moral state of the person. When personal freedom and the ability to make moral decisions mature in the

child, he or she can choose the good and decide the place of God in his or her life.

Original sin sets up a force toward "strange gods" of pride, selfishness, power, and injustice while grace sets up an opposing force of humility, truth, goodness, love, and justice.

The Power of Grace: Redeemed Human Nature

Grace

The power of grace that helps us to change evil to good begins with single acts. Individual people can involve others of goodwill, who in turn influence groups and states and entire countries. The power of evil can be stemmed by the power of good. The power of evil is often part of systems or structures erected by human beings, and it is human beings who can change them. We are largely responsible for the evil in the world today, whether it be isolated acts of evil or systemic evil embedded in the structures of society. It is our responsibility to bring good where evil is present, to "be our brother's [and sister's] keeper." In situations of poverty, war, and disease, innocent people cannot help themselves because they do not have the resources to do so. Disciples who have the heart and mind of Jesus will do all they can to be brother and sister to those in need.

Disciples are not alone in their efforts. God's grace is present in every desire to do good and to bring peace. Grace is especially effective through the Eucharistic liturgy and the sacraments. Here we have direct experiences of God in powerful ways that bring about what the sacrament symbolizes. Eucharist gives thanks and nourishes; Baptism cleanses; Reconciliation harmonizes relationships; Anointing comforts and strengthens; Confirmation verifies faith; Matrimony unites husband and wife. Grace is present in the loving support of others, in the opportunities for good that come our way, in the gifts of life around us, and in the church through its many ministries. There is no limit to the ways grace assists us to change the patterns, systems, and structures of evil in our day.

Redeemed Human Nature

Each Easter Vigil service takes the community through the experiences of light and dark. In the darkness of the night a flame is lit. The service dramatically symbolizes the journey from darkness of death in sin to the glorious light found in Christ and in his resurrection. The death and resurrection of Christ become the new life journey of each disciple. This spiritual reality is brought home in the cultural setting of each local church celebrating the Easter Vigil.

My first Easter Vigil in New Orleans was infused with the smells and sounds of the city. Just one block from the banks of the river stands the French-style St. Louis Cathedral. The vigil service began with the worshiping community gathering in the alley separating the presbytery from the cathedral. A recent rain freshened the foul smells of alleys used and misused by street people, and combined with the soft smell of sweet-olive-tree blossoms and the odors of stale grease from nearby restaurants. Hollow-sounding fog horns from passing ships and the jazz music of street musicians formed a musical background to the service. The sounds and smells of the city brought the blessings and ills of the city's people — all of humanity — to the service. The archbishop lit the dry sticks that immediately leapt into bright flames. It seemed the very wood jumped to new life and was eager to be passed to the waiting candles of the community. "Jesus Christ, yesterday, today and forever," said the celebrant as he marked the Easter candle. The procession moved back into the cathedral on the centuries-old flagstone walk, passed tourists who were taken with the spectacle of a candlelight procession. I was proud of my candle and its little light and of the combined lights of my companions. We knew we had a light in the darkness — a light fueled by the life and death of Jesus. That was good news! The community was proclaiming the insurmountable power of life that Jesus brought to each believer, a power renewed over and over in each Easter remembrance, in each Eucharistic celebration, and in the sacraments, especially the sacrament of Reconciliation. The community once inside the church broke out in joyous Easter alleluias as the choir led them in the ancient Gregorian chants that took worshipers back to the early history of the Christian community. Time and peoples and places were all brought together in one worshiping experience. The mystery of redemption was thus continued, as it is continued in each new group gathered to light its Easter candles.

In the midst of a city with its personal and social sins, the grace of Christ is proclaimed anew. No matter the crime rate, the poverty, and the prejudice, Jesus is choosing to be with his people. Easter is a high point of celebration and joy, but it is also a challenge to each believer that new life must be brought to each location. Grace is there to change the patterns of crime, to erase poverty and prejudice ("Eracism," says the bumper-sticker), to stop drug trafficking, and to find a job and home for anyone who wants one. Easter affirms these deepest of desires of the worshipers and motivates them not to give up and to try again, to find better strategies to change the systems. Most of all Easter invites all to conversion in their hearts. Once personal change is effected, the structures of evil have to yield because parishioners again experience Jesus with them. Immanuel is with his people and brings light out of darkness.

Conclusion

We can take surveys of contemporary cities, countries, and nations and see evidence of sin in every location. The environment of the earth itself has been tainted by human structures and systems of injustice and greed. Each of these has been constructed through the acts of individuals who chose evil rather than good, who chose "strange gods" rather than the real God. People have left a heritage of sin that influences everyone — a heritage called original sin. Yet, because we are redeemed by a loving God who sent his son to rescue humanity, sin does not have ultimate power. The power of Jesus Christ, of good, truth, love, peace, and justice, overpowers any contrary forces. The grace of God present in and through the church, in the goodness of the earth and humanity, still overcomes the power of evil. Easter gives the impetus to conversion from evil and to a new life where love and justice reign supreme.

Notes

1. Richard M. Gula, *Reason Informed by Faith* (New York: Paulist Press, 1989), 102.

2. Karl H. Peschke, *Christian Ethics: Moral Theology in the Light of Vatican II* (Alcester, S.D.: C. Goodliffe Neale, 1989), 165.

3. Jon Sobrino, S.J., "Evil and Hope: Spiritual and Pastoral Perspectives" (plenary talk at CTSA convention, New York, 1995).

4. "Bishops Discuss Land Mines and Liturgy," *America* (July 15, 1995): 8.

5. See chapter 3 for a full explanation of the fundamental option. The fundamental option is defined there as an act that establishes the person's moral stance toward God in terms of a basic choice for good or evil.

6. The issue of erroneous conscience arises here. The objective moral wrong is clearly present, but less clear is the subjective moral wrong. A confessor with the penitent is more able to judge the subjective guilt accompanying the moral evil. See chapter 7 on conscience.

7. Louis Janssens, "Ontic Evil and Moral Evil," in *Readings in Moral Theology*, vol. 1, ed. Charles E. Curran and Richard A. McCormick, S.J., 40–93 (New York: Paulist Press, 1979).

8. Gula, *Reason Informed by Faith*, 102.

9. See ibid., 111.

10. Frank J. Macchiarola, ed., *Caring for America's Children* (Montpelier, Vt.: Capital City Press, 1989).

11. Josef Fuchs, S.J., "Structures of Sin and Sin," in *Moral Demands and Personal Obligations* (Washington, D.C.: Georgetown University Press, 1993), 63–73.

12. Gula, *Reason Informed by Faith*, 106.

Chapter 6

MORAL AUTHORITY
AND MORAL NORMS

What do these people have in common: Caesar, Alexander the Great, Benedict, Constantine, Gregory the Great, Joan of Arc, Napoleon, Martin Luther, Clara Barton, Eleanor Roosevelt, Charles de Gaulle, Dwight Eisenhower, Winston Churchill, Adolph Hitler, Margaret Thatcher, Bill Clinton? All of these renowned people have been leaders at some time in history. They were powerful men and women possessing great authority in the political sphere, in religious movements, and in social movements. Some, however, were not worthy leaders or could not be called moral leaders in a positive sense; others, like Benedict, Clara Barton, and Eleanor Roosevelt, led people to effect tremendous amounts of good and growth.

The leaders listed had extensive influence that came from power they possessed, often not because of their own merit but because people elected them, people with influence delegated or appointed them, or soldiers backed them. In order to exercise authority one must have the power to do so. There are many types of authority, from parental authority to religious authority, each one being responsible for moral guidance. The church, through the magisterium, offers moral guidance in its moral norms, public pronouncements, and pastoral care. This chapter will examine power and the role of authority in moral formation. The correlate of authority is response, something that will also be discussed in this chapter.

Whether persons in authority use their power in government, military, or religious leadership, authority is derived from the power of the people and ultimately from one source of power, God. All leaders only share in the fullness of God's power. In *Pacem in Terris*, Pope John XXIII said: "Indeed, since it is the power to command according to right reason, authority must derive its obligatory force from the moral order, which in turn has God for its first source and final end" (46).

Moral authority differs from elected, conquered, or delegated authority. The governor of a state may be elected by the majority of voters, but that does not always assure the governor of moral authority. Pope John Paul II in *Evangelium Vitae* describes this contemporary situation in government:

> [I]t is easy to see that without an objective moral grounding not even democracy is capable of ensuring a stable peace, especially since peace which is not built upon values of the dignity of every individual and of solidarity between all people frequently proves to be illusory. Even in participatory systems of government the regulation of interest often occurs to the advantage of the most powerful, since they are the ones most capable of maneuvering not only the levers of power but also of shaping the formation of consensus. In such a situation, democracy easily becomes an empty word. (70)

People who are not elected may hold greater moral authority if they are recognized for their integrity and their ability to stand for ideals and to withstand the pressure of counterforces. This was the case of Martin Luther King Jr., whose moral authority in the realm of faith and social justice was widely acknowledged. People of diverse religions understood his message, accepted it, and were motivated by Dr. King's words to join the efforts to achieve civil rights. King had moral authority. How did he, and others, gain moral authority? What are the parameters of this authority? Who is bound by it? Answers to these questions will be important for understanding the type of authority exercised by leaders of the faith community whose duty it is to provide moral guidance to its members. This chapter will begin with a consideration of moral authority and then focus on its corollary, moral guidance, which can be furnished by one possessing moral authority.

Moral Authority

Moral Authority and the Faith Community

Moral authority is attained in several ways. Consider these situations. In Jim's house, youngsters have to check with their parents about movie ratings before they attend the latest film. Kristi knows it is her turn to be with her elderly grandmother this weekend because a schedule of care has been agreed upon by the family. Tony didn't go with his friends for a pizza after baseball practice because his dad said he was to come right home. The seventh-grade teacher was called out of the classroom during a history test; David could have easily cheated but chose not to because he knew his teacher had held up honesty as a high value for her students. Each of these families, parents, and teachers exercises moral authority. Jim as a parent and the seventh-grade teacher, by the nature of their roles, have moral authority to form the younger generation. Men and women have moral authority when they become parents; they are then responsible for their children's moral formation. Parents delegate their authority to teachers, who are to instill the moral values of the parents in their students. Jim, Kristi, Tony, and David knew the moral authority of their parents and teachers, to whom they chose to respond.

Some people receive moral authority when they take on the responsibilities of an office such as that of president, mayor, or principal of a school. People expect moral rectitude and ensuing moral authority from these people. Police officers are to enforce laws and protect citizens; doctors and nurses are to save lives and heal people; social workers are to help those in need of social assistance; tax assessors are to be honest in their assessments. Each person holding an office or job in public trust has the confidence of the public that the task will be carried out correctly and honestly and that authority will be exercised appropriately. Some offices, however, possess greater moral authority than others. When an office is very important, public trust is increased and greater moral authority is expected, as in the case of clergy, police officers, government officials, medical personnel, and teachers. The expectations of the public endow officeholders with moral authority insofar as it pertains to their job or office. It is then highly offensive to learn of corruption in police departments, to find government officials taking bribes and voting according to the interests of lobbyists, and to learn of teachers violating their students. Public outcry about medical malpractice voices the deep disappointment of the public when trust has been violated by a member of the medical profession. Each of these cases expresses a violation of trust and failure to provide what was justly expected: moral integrity and moral authority.

The public expects more of its leaders than of ordinary citizens. We need only recall the amount of press given presidents and public officials regarding sexual improprieties, Watergate, Whitewater, and misappropriation of public funds. Citizens expect high moral standards of their leaders. They are to exercise moral authority not only by their office but also by the moral integrity of their lives.

These same expectations of moral rectitude pertain to religious leaders such as priests, ministers, rabbis, and those in pastoral ministry. As leaders of the faith community, they hold moral authority and are expected, by right of their office, to provide moral guidance by their words and by the example of their lives. While moral integrity is a calling for all who follow Christ, it is especially desired in the leaders of the faith community. Moral uprightness is expected of those with moral authority. The church recognizes this expectation and addresses it in the diaconate ordination. The bishop admonishes the candidate about moral integrity: "By your life and character you will give witness to your brothers and sisters in faith that God must be loved above all else, and that it is he whom you serve in others." Later in the ordination rite to priesthood, the bishop says, "Meditate on the law of God, believe what you read, teach what you believe, and put into practice what you teach."

Moral authority carries with it moral responsibility in proportion to the importance of the office. Many have carried this responsibility to an outstanding degree and have paid for it with their lives. History is replete with the stories of countless religious leaders who have exercised powerful moral leadership in the church. Consider some recent religious leaders whose moral leadership is globally acknowledged. Cardinal Mindszenty of Hungary confronted the communist regime and witnessed to its injustices for more than twenty years as a house prisoner. Archbishop Romero was assassinated because he took a public stand against the atrocities of the government toward the poor of El Salvador. This was followed in 1989 with the martyrdom of six Jesuit priests and two women, murdered because of their social-justice work in behalf of the poor and their criticism of the government for its unjust policies. Father Dominic Tran Dinh Thu, founder of a Vietnamese religious order, was imprisoned for ten years under the communist leadership of North Vietnam for no stated reason but ostensibly for his staunch defense of the faith and encouragement to the laity to be firm in their beliefs. In similar style, the exiled archbishop of Saigon, Francisco Nguyen Van Thaun, was imprisoned for twelve years, nine of which were spent in solitary confinement. *Still today* the bishops of many countries take on the formidable task of stopping injustice wherever a government oversteps its bounds.

The most effective moral leaders are those who also witness with the personal moral integrity of their lives. Because they lead lives of moral integrity, their moral leadership is the stronger. Their moral authority challenges government structures and political movements, rights social wrongs, assists the needy and helpless, and is a beacon of hope to Christian disciples. We have seen that moral authority is necessary and important because we need guidance from competent leaders. There are several ways one acquires moral authority: when one assumes a role of authority, as one grows in personal integrity, or when one earns it. Leaders in the church, for example, gain moral authority when they assume the role of bishop.

Moral Authority and the Magisterium

Moral authority in the church is found in the gospel, through personal moral integrity, and in all the members by right of Baptism in the Holy Spirit. Moral authority is present in a special way in the magisterium.

The magisterium is comprised of bishops, cardinals, and the pope. As leaders of the church founded by Jesus Christ, their primary task is to teach by communicating and interpreting the Word of God for the present day. Just as all members of the church possess moral authority, so all members share with the leaders of the church their primary task of teaching the Christian message. This task is focused in the work of teachers, catechists, and formation personnel, whether lay, clergy, or religious.

Moral authority is shared with the magisterium when members of the church take on roles of responsibility. Leaders of a parish, members of a pastoral council, and catechists have moral authority. The decisions and tasks carried out on the local level of a parish affect the wider church on the diocesan and national level. We see moral authority at work when a diocesan synod is called, in the laity when bishops consult them about specific issues, and when conferences focus on the scriptures. Those church members who speak up for moral issues in the public arena have the moral authority of their Baptism and can rely on the moral authority of the community to support them in their stand.

The members of the magisterium have a specific role to play and have the moral authority to carry out that role. Besides being teachers, these persons are bound to be faithful to the tradition passed on from the first community of disciples through each succeeding generation. They are to encourage the study of scripture and the teachings of the church, as well as scholarship in theology. In preserving the tradition of the church, they rely on the practices of the church, the decisions of church councils, and the writings of the popes. Each of these sources of tradition emerged from an understanding of revelation, the practice of the faith, and the beliefs of ordinary people in local parishes. Eventually these traditions were accepted by the entire church. Just so, the moral traditions of the church emerged from revelation such as found in the Ten Commandments and the two commandments of love and in the practical application of the faith in the daily lives of ordinary Christians. These practices eventually were embodied in moral norms (which will be discussed more fully later in the chapter).

Moral norms pertain to specific teachings such as those regarding just wages, the rights of workers, family life and marriage, responsible care of resources and the environment, governments, and freedom. It is difficult to know all of the material contained in the moral tradition of the church. Theologians and church leaders study, research, and teach the moral tradition of the church, but it is the specific duty of the local pastor to keep parishioners informed about the moral tradition through his homilies and teaching.

While all magisterial teachings must be treated with respect and attention, not all moral teachings have the same level of importance. Dogmas and the decrees of councils carry more weight than the weekly talks given by the pope to the visitors at St. Peter's. Encyclicals hold a prominent place in the teachings of the church. There are about three hundred encyclicals that detail the popes' teachings on moral matters, doctrinal issues, and church matters. Most encyclical letters are addressed to "All People of Goodwill" and not just to members of the Roman Catholic Church. Pope John Paul II believes his moral leadership extends beyond the boundaries of one body of believers. However, the pope requires assistance in carrying out his tasks as a leader for all people.

The pope cannot possibly administrate the extensive undertakings of the church alone. Various branches of administration called the Roman curia conduct the daily functioning of the church. Residing in Rome, the Roman curia

> fulfills its duty in his [the pope's] name and by his authority for the good and the service of the Churches; it consists of the Secretariat of State or the Papal Secretariat, congregations, tribunals and other institutions, whose structure and competency are defined in special law (canon 360). The Roman curia is the complex of departments and institutes which assist the Roman Pontiff in the exercise of his supreme pastoral function for the

good and service of the universal Church and of the particular churches, by which the unity of faith and communion of the people of God is strengthened and the mission is promoted which is proper to the Church in the world.[1]

The departments of administration in Rome are called "congregations" (not to be confused with religious congregations or orders) or Roman curia. Nine such congregations oversee matters pertaining to doctrine, canonization of saints, Oriental churches, bishops, sacraments and worship, propagation of the faith, religious life, clergy, and Catholic education. The pontifical councils and tribunals address the pastoral concerns of the church, areas where moral issues surface and are discussed (see table 2).

Table 2
The Congregations, Pontifical Councils, and Tribunals

The Congregations

1. Congregation for the Doctrine of the Faith
2. Congregation for the Causes of Saints
3. Congregation for Oriental Churches
4. Congregation for Bishops
5. Congregation for Divine Worship and the Discipline of the Sacraments
6. Congregation for the Evangelization of People or Propagation of the Faith
7. Congregation for Institutes of Consecrated Life and Societies of Apostolic Life
8. Congregation for the Clergy
9. Congregation for Catholic Education

Tribunals

1. Apostolic Penitentiary
2. Supreme Tribunal of the Apostolic Signatura
3. Tribunal of the Roman Rota

Pontifical Councils

1. Pontifical Council for the Laity
2. Pontifical Council for Promoting Christian Unity
3. Pontifical Council for the Family
4. Pontifical Council for Justice and Peace
5. Pontifical Council "Cor Unum"
6. Pontifical Council for the Pastoral Care of Migrants & Itinerant People
7. Pontifical Council for the Pastoral Assistance to Health Care Workers
8. Pontifical Council for Interpretation of Legal Texts
9. Pontifical Council for Dialogue with Non-Believers
10. Pontifical Council for Culture
11. Pontifical Council for Social Communications

Moral Guidance

When we have a problem, most often we turn to family and friends for support and for moral guidance. These people know us and usually understand the situation with which we are coping because they know the context and the people involved. Each of us knows those faith-filled wisdom people to whom we can turn for guidance such as a former teacher or maybe a grandparent. The local church has resources from which we draw wisdom and receive guidance. The pastor and pastoral ministers of a parish are available to offer insight, information, support, and moral guidance along with pastoral counseling. The parish staff relies on the input of the bishop for the setting of policies and for an interpretation of church teaching in a specific moral situation. This is particularly true in medical dilemmas, in legal disputes, in election years when one has to sort out the merits of a party platform or the stand of an individual candidate. Sometimes politics confuses the moral issues; at other times we have trouble sorting out the morally right thing to do in a dilemma that arises at work. Raising children today presents unique challenges and questions not faced by past generations.

Beyond the local parish and the diocese, most countries have organizations of church leaders who meet regularly to discuss moral issues and offer a direction to resolve moral problems. In the United States the NCCB (National Council of Catholic Bishops) serves this role. The church also has offices that focus on specific issues confronting the universal church.

Moral guidance is provided for the worldwide church through the various Roman offices, each delegated to carry out the church's mission. The work of the Roman curia is based on research, dialogue, and study. The Roman curia exercises administrative leadership insofar as it shares in the teaching ministry of the pope. Its main role is to assist us when moral questions arise and the church needs more clarification regarding an issue. The documents produced by each office bear the signature of its leader and are sometimes accompanied with a statement of the pope's approval. At times moral norms are defined through one of the congregations, most often by the Congregation for the Doctrine of the Faith. The norms can be included in decrees, in instructions, in declarations, and in norms themselves. Sometimes official responses are published in reply to particular questions, for example the ability of deacons to solemnize marriages. Each of the documents addresses particular situations that require clarification, doctrinal explanation, recommendations, or directive norms. The documents may interpret existing laws or offer guidelines for application of certain principles.

Moral Traditions of the Church: Official Teaching

Official teaching on the moral life is given by the chief teachers of the church, the magisterium. This teaching can be given in various ways depending upon the importance of the teaching: ordinary or extraordinary. Some teaching does not require that the pope and bishops meet as a body but can still be given by the pope in union with all bishops throughout the world. A teaching given by the pope without official declaration, or by a bishop for his diocese, is considered part of the ordinary magisterium. Encyclicals or exhortations upholding respect for life and the motherhood of Mary are part of the ordinary magisterium. Encyclicals and apostolic letters sent by the pope to the universal church are also part of the ordinary magisterium. Usually on Wednesdays, the pope addresses the crowds of visitors to the Vatican. These talks, as well as those given on his many trips to various countries, are considered part of the ordinary magisterium. An extraordinary teaching pertains to matters of faith or morals and is publicly declared as being an extraordinary teaching (see table 3).

Table 3
Types of Moral
Teaching

From the Magisterium:

- Ordinary

- Extraordinary

Level of Teaching:

- Infallible

- Noninfallible

Since there are various levels of teaching, how would one know the importance of a teaching? The bishops of Vatican II specified the differences between the teachings in the document *Lumen Gentium* (see no. 25). The nature of the teaching and the importance given the teaching can be determined through the manner in which it is delivered. Those teachings concerned with faith or morals can be declared infallible or accepted as noninfallible. Infallible teachings can be declared by the pope or by the pope in union with the bishops. If the teaching is issued by the pope it is said to be ex cathedra, meaning it comes "from the chair," from the pope who sits on the "chair of Peter," whom he succeeds as leader of the faith community. This extraordinary teaching must meet rigid standards for truth and have no possibility of error now or in the future. For these reasons there have been very few teachings declared infallible. The last two teachings declared infallible were the dogmas of the Immaculate Conception (1854) and the Assumption (1950), although other teachings are considered infallible by the nature of their truth. These teachings belong to the ordinary magisterium, which includes some teachings on moral theology. Some theologians maintain there are elements of infallibility contained in the universal magisterium that should be publicly declared infallible, such as "respect for life." Because they fear moral relativism and a weakening of moral standards in society, these theologians would prefer that some moral statements be publicly declared infallible. A declaration of infallibility would not change the truth of the teaching, but by extending the mantle of church authority, the truth-claims might be better substantiated.

Noninfallible teachings contain truth and important values that the magisterium wants to uphold. While noninfallible teachings are open to change when new developments in theology, knowledge, and technology are made known, they do contain the best knowledge available to church leaders at the time and uphold values important for the practice of the faith. The values and views they contain are so important that believers are to treat these teachings with respect, an openness of mind and heart, and a willingness to do all possible to bring the values into actuality. A loyal response to noninfallible teachings is called "submission of will and of mind" or "religious assent" (*Lumen Gentium* 25). This means that we believe the Spirit guides the church in truth, so we will make every effort to appropriate the teachings of the church. Francis A. Sullivan, who has studied and written on religious submission, says: "As I understand it, then, to give the required *obsequium religiosum* to the teaching of the ordinary magisterium means to make an honest and sustained effort to overcome any contrary opinion I might have, and to achieve a sincere assent of my mind to this teaching."[2]

Most moral teachings are noninfallible. Some examples include

mandates on justice and mercy, political involvement, economic reform to grant help to the poor and oppressed, and universal efforts
for peace, all of which are presented in the encyclicals and letters issued by the popes beginning with Leo XIII. Noninfallible teachings
include moral norms: sexual norms, norms on social issues, directives
on medical ethics, and business ethics.

The minimalist attitude toward moral norms is to "get by" and
not commit a sin. This attitude can influence the outlook toward noninfallible teachings: "If a teaching is not so important (noninfallible),
I can make up my own mind about following it, and I do not have
to take it too seriously." With this mentality, a person would disregard all but infallible teaching and consider only directives coming
from the pope himself. Moral guidance coming from a bishop or
pastor would be inferior to that of the pope and could therefore be
discounted. Those who want to be disciples of Jesus will give serious
attention to the successor of Peter and to the magisterium and will
consider the nature of the teaching, its content, and the values being endorsed. Such disciples will not have a minimalist attitude but
rather will view moral teachings in terms of growth in love, justice,
and service. Their question is, What are all the things I can do to be
a faithful follower of Jesus? The application of Jesus' teachings to
modern-day needs is found in the teachings of the church and so are
to be taken to heart and made real in the life of believers.

Preserving Moral Values of the Church

Moral teachings embody moral values of the church. In order to preserve moral values from one generation to the next, the values are
codified in moral norms. The norm "Honor your father and mother"
highlights the values of respect, love, and care for parents and all
just authorities. Paying a just wage to employees is based on the values of justice and dignity of the human person. Participation in the
political process emphasizes the values of rights and freedom of the
individual, responsibility for government, and the common good.

Moral Norms as Embodying Values

Each moral principle and moral norm is derived from a foundation
of value. In the case of the Christian, the value should be traceable
to the values of Jesus as they are applied to today's world. Norms
are not to be obeyed merely for the sake of obedience: "If I obey, I
will be found good, will be approved, and will go to heaven." While
these reasons may be worthy ones, they do not go far enough. The

ultimate value of moral norms is to assist one to follow Jesus in a community of freedom and love. In obeying moral norms, the disciple tries to take on Jesus' mentality, his way of life, and his way of relating and loving. When obeyed consciously, moral norms can educate us in moral values that become our own.

Moral norms serve as guides. Based on Christian wisdom, reflection, study, and prayer by those who have gone before us, moral norms are lights that show a direction to travel. This is especially helpful when trying to make moral decisions and the way is dim because there are so many confusing factors to consider. Moral norms are instructive and informative. Once one has learned as a child not to cheat, not to steal, and to tell the truth, these instructions are knit in one's bones. Teaching a child moral norms makes them part of the child's moral sinew, which builds strong moral character. There is a sense of certainty and well-being when one knows that one is doing the right thing, not just because a rule is being obeyed but because an instruction has now moved to the "heart." The disciple senses from inner knowledge the right thing to do.

It is important that Christians teach their children not only the moral traditions of the church but also the stories of the preservation of that tradition by believers and leaders of the church. Moral traditions and moral values can also be preserved in the standards and norms of society that are called civil law. Moreover, attitudes and modes of morality are sustained in the traditions of a culture, a region, and even a country. For example, from its foundation the United States has fought for freedom and rights of individual citizens and is today known for its stands based on freedom and rights of individuals. The Native Americans witness to the value of the earth and its environment. Some cultures, like the African and Vietnamese cultures, preserve the tradition of strong family bonds and community life. We must consider societal norms if we are to obtain a full picture of the moral tradition.

Societal Norms

> This is a government of law not of men.
>
> — Thomas Jefferson
> (above courthouse entrance,
> New Orleans)

Civil law is to be objective and is to serve the good of all citizens, not bent to the will of any one person. Through civil law government tries to address the social problems that arise in the cities, country-side, and suburban areas. The "laws of the land," or civil laws, strive to help every citizen whether the law comes in the form of taxation, speed limits for motor vehicles, or curfews for youngsters. Sometimes called "positive human law," civil laws are established to protect cit-izens and to achieve the common good. H. C. Gardiner summarizes the purpose of civil law:

> Law serves the common good in two ways. First, it positively advances the common good (as in establishing minimum wages, for example); second, it can forbid what would injure the com-mon good. To perform this second task effectively, the public authority must have power to penalize those who violate the common good. Legitimate authority, in other words, has puni-tive power, which it has not only the right but also the duty to exercise when necessary for the common good.[3]

Civil law, like moral law, embodies values that are to be upheld, maintained, and enforced. There are, however, differences between civil law coming from legislative bodies and moral norms coming from religious authority (table 4). Civil laws may manifest moral and religious values of the faith community, but this is not always the case. History shows divergence between civil government and religious leadership on many issues, from present-day abortion leg-islation, to seizure of property, capital punishment, military service in unjust wars, taxation without representation, and imprisonment without due cause. The pope has recently spoken about the moral dilemmas Christians face when moral and civil law are at odds. He said that the purpose of civil law is different and more limited than that of moral norms. The civil law cannot take the place of con-science. The only laws civil authority can dictate are those related to the common good of people, the recognition and defense of people's fundamental rights, and the promotion of peace and public morality (*Evangelium Vitae* 71).

While civil authority is limited, it nevertheless ought to uphold moral values that undergird the responsibilities just mentioned. We frequently find that rather than opposing traditional religious values, civil law embodies moral norms and values of the church. This is es-pecially true of most of the Ten Commandments, whose values have been supported by civil legislation.

An age-old tradition of the church is the principle, "All just laws and all legitimate authority are to be obeyed." Obedience itself must

---

Table 4
Laws and Moral Norms

- Civil Law

- Moral Norms

  1. Formal Norms

  2. Material Norms

- Moral Absolutes

---

be examined, if it is to be a virtue. When obedience becomes over-obedience, people obey without questioning the purpose of the law or the values it endorses. They obey simply because it is the law, or because they fear what will happen if they do not obey. Such was the case of the SS men supervising and controlling the Nazi death camps during World War II. Lieutenant William Calley, an American army officer during the Vietnam War, learned that the military courts do not uphold indiscriminate violation of human rights and moral codes during war. Civil laws must be respected and examined, and then a decision about compliance or noncompliance must be made. Because the law serves the good of everyone in the community, not just individual good, one cannot simply take the law into one's own hands. Decisions about obedience to civil law require maturity and require the exercise of personal conscience. (The topic of conscience will be addressed more fully in chapter 7.)

Moral Norms

Disciples of Jesus receive moral guidance from many sources, one being moral norms promulgated through the leaders of the church. As stated above, these norms reflect the values, wisdom, and understanding of Jesus as applied to today's world. Values that Jesus emphasized were compassion, forgiveness, and love. Wisdom is needed to recognize and be able to choose good with the understanding of Jesus.

Depending upon the type of matter under consideration, moral norms can carry more or less weight. The life of a human being carries great moral weight. "Do not kill" not only forbids taking of human life but in a positive sense calls for respect and care for human life from its beginning to ending stages (see *Evangelium Vi-*

tae 3). Moral norms can be expressed in negative terms, "Thou shalt not...," or in positive terms, as in "Care for the poor, weak, and helpless."

Unlike civil norms, moral norms appeal to conscience and the freedom to follow the way of Jesus. Moral norms exceed minimal requirements and strict justice; they require Jesus' perspective to understand them: "Forgive your enemies; do good to those who offend you." Many of the norms found in the New Testament, particularly in the Sermon on the Mount, are general in nature; they do not give specific directives. They are ideals toward which one must strive. Such norms are called formal norms (see table 4). The law of love, "Love God above all things and your neighbor as yourself," is a formal norm, as are the Ten Commandments. These norms and the law of love from Jesus undergird all other norms, particularly specific moral norms.

When a moral norm addresses specific behaviors, it is called a material norm. This type of norm is a further specification of the law of love and gives concrete directions about how this law is to be interpreted. The precepts of the church governing observance of holy days, fasting, and confession of sins are material norms. Norms on sexuality and social and political issues are material norms. Besides having a basis in the law of love, these norms are also derived from an interpretation of natural law. Frequently, material norms, such as those on medical and social ethics, have a lengthy tradition that is updated by the magisterium. Recently the pope and bishops have spoken against capital punishment and euthanasia. This teaching is an interpretation of the formal norm to "respect life" and an interpretation of biblical teachings on responsibility for human life. There has been a long tradition of respect for life, but this updated teaching specifies a general teaching for a current situation and specifies how it is to be applied today. When material norms are issued, the magisterium frequently recounts the tradition upon which its teaching stands: scripture, natural law, encyclicals, and the writings of outstanding theologians such as Thomas Aquinas.

Moral Maturity, Obedience, and Dissent

Moral maturity can be seen at each stage of development in the human life-cycle. A child of four can act more mature than its age and then act like a baby; an adolescent might act one minute like a thirteen-year-old and then like a sixteen-year-old. Maturity can only be defined based on the unique context of the person being considered. However, most often maturity is equated with adulthood. Today psychologists find that age does not define adulthood. Someone still dependent on institutions and family for support at age thirty may not have experienced the full social and psychological responsibilities of adulthood.

Moral maturity correlates with physical and psychological development, experiences, interpretations of those experiences, cognitive development, and self-knowledge. The research of Lawrence Kohlberg traces the connections between cognition and moral development, while Erik Erikson demonstrates the effects of socialization on psychological maturation.[4] Both argue that psychological and moral maturity are not separate from one's social environment, such as the family or society in which one lives.

The morally mature Christian will reflect on teachings of the church. Given the importance of moral teachings, they are to be studied with openness, with respect, and with a sincere desire to appropriate them in our lives. On occasion, we may find that a specific moral norm does not serve the purpose for which it was intended in a particular case. This being no small matter, a decision requires moral maturity, faith, an informed conscience, and a sincere desire to follow Christ in order to decide in this case not to obey a moral norm.

The church is open to truth as it is made known through human research and study. Mistakes have been made throughout history regarding moral norms that discriminated against groups of people such as African-Americans, slaves, women, the poor, and those with disabilities or diseases. Those people who realize greater truth than is revealed in a moral norm serve the church when they point this out to members of the magisterium, to pastoral leaders, and to those who can effect change. Material norms are noninfallible in nature, and so there is need to move from truth known at a given time to greater truth that is known later. It is a service to the church to assist the leaders with knowledge that is specific to a certain discipline and that may not be fully understood or known by the hierarchy. This type of service by the laity can be seen in a positive sense of "truth-seeking" together with church leaders. Medical research has been helpful in understanding methods of natural family planning and end-of-life issues such as those regarding nutrition and hydration. The economics pastoral issued by the U.S. bishops in 1986 could not have been as effective without the input of economists, business leaders, and finance experts.

When there is resistance to sharing and dialogue, when there is a lack of openness to moral norms, some will dissent from church teaching. Others will dissent for justifiable intellectual reasons, hoping that through the dissent greater truth will emerge. Because assent to or acceptance of moral norms is a matter of conscience, dissent is a significant stand that not only affects the individual dissenting from a teaching but when made public can affect members of the community. Confusion, divisiveness, even scandal can be caused when the dissenter is a well-known person, like the pastor. The moral burden is on the one who dissents, while the presumption of truth is on the side of the magisterium (*Lumen Gentium* 25). Moral maturity is needed to discern difficult issues of obedience and disobedience, whether it be to civil law or moral norms.

Conclusion

The role of authority in morality is significant. Those in authority who exercise moral leadership can be officials in government or in the church; more often moral authority is most influential in relationships of love. Parents, teachers, and family members are those in love relationships with children and are those who have the greatest influence on their moral development and on the formation of their consciences. The responsibility of persons in authority is tremendous because it must be exercised not only for the good of an individual but for the common good. Church teachings guide leaders and members of the faith community in exercising their moral leadership. Assent to the authorities and to moral norms is not the goal of Christian morality, but they are guides to the end that is love of God, self, and neighbor, as stated in the law of love.

Notes

1. *Catholic Directory* (New Providence, N.J.: P. J. Kenedy and Sons, 1995), xxxi.

2. Francis A. Sullivan, *Magisterium: Teaching Authority in the Catholic Church* (New York: Paulist Press, 1983), 164.

3. H. C. Gardiner, "Censorship," in *Catholic Encyclopedia* (New York: McGraw Hill, 1967), 3:391.

4. See Lawrence Kohlberg, *The Philosophy of Moral Development,* vol. 1 (San Francisco: Harper and Row, 1981); and Erik H. Erikson, *Childhood and Society* (New York: W. W. Norton, 1963).

Chapter 7

CONSCIENCE

Winnie the Pooh loved honey. One day when he heard bees buzzing around a tree he knew there was honey in that tree and he had to have some. He spotted a hole in the tree trunk to which the bees flew to deposit more honey. Winnie waited patiently until the bees had seemingly all left for their morning flight in the clover field. With the taste of honey already in his mouth, Winnie quickly climbed the tree. His mouth was watering as he neared the hole. Throwing caution to the wind, Winnie immediately thrust his head into the hole to gulp some of the precious golden food. With a loud howl and a violent jerk Winnie withdrew his head in pain. The bees inside the hole had stung his snout and continued to attack him as he scampered down the tree and ran far from the bees. Did Winnie feel remorseful after stealing honey from the bees? Indeed not! Did Winnie have any regrets for trying to steal the honey? Of course not! The only thing he regretted and felt badly about was his pain. On his next honey-stealing escapade he would simply have to be a bit more cautious and time things a little better.

Debra and her mother-in-law, Mrs. Grayson, had been at odds ever since she told Debra she could no longer baby-sit two-year-old Jessica. Mrs. Grayson had decided to take a part-time job that would get her out of the house and provide a little income. Debra felt the job was not necessary because the Graysons had more than enough money on which to retire. She felt Mrs. Grayson was selfish and unwilling to help out, especially since she knew Debra and her husband were having a hard time finding a good baby-sitter. When asked by a friend why Mrs. Grayson no longer baby-sat for Jessica, Debra, in anger, made a comment that hinted at sexual abuse. Debra knew the accusation was false, but she did not correct the statement. In a short time, her friend had spread the word that Mrs. Grayson sexually abused her granddaughter. When Mrs. Grayson heard of this, she and her husband were devastated. They spoke to Debra, who apologized profusely with many tears. She realized, too late, that she had damaged the reputation of her mother-in-law, that she had done something terribly wrong that she deeply regretted.

James won a lottery jackpot that landed him a check for three million dollars. He could not believe his good fortune! Even after taxes were paid, James knew he had a sizable amount on which to live well and to care for his poor and aging parents, who had depleted their savings on medical bills. He contacted an investment broker who helped him decide about stock and bond investments that would net him the most for his money. The broker seemed to ignore James's parents in the financial planning. This surprised James, who in conscience felt bound to care for his parents, especially now that he could afford to do so.

What made the responses of Winnie the Pooh, Debra, and James so different? One could see differences in how responsible each felt. Debra felt responsible for her actions and admitted guilt. Winnie the Pooh did not. James felt responsible for his parents. Winnie the Pooh acted out of instinct, while Debra and James acted out of human thought processes that allowed them to reflect on past actions, enact actions in the present, and plan other actions for the future.

As human beings, James and Debra could foresee the consequences of their actions because they had specific mental abilities Winnie the Pooh did not have. They had a sense of time and could make judgments after reflecting on the consequences of their actions. They knew their actions would affect the lives of others to whom they were bound in a social network. In this case, Winnie the Pooh had no care for other creatures or a sense of responsibility for them because one of his primary instinctual needs was to care for himself. The most stark contrast between Winnie, Debra, and James was the presence of conscience that raised Debra and James's awareness to a moral level, while Winnie did not reflect morally, but rather out of instinctual knowledge learned from past experiences. One could object that Winnie was an animal who, of course, did not have a conscience. But consider the times human beings have been described as "animals" because of their inhumane behavior and the times animals have shown great responsibility for their own offspring, flock, or herd and for their human owners and loved ones. What then is the difference between truly human behavior that includes conscience as one of the definers of "human" and behavior that seems antithetical to the good of human beings? Is conscience the definer of "human" behavior? What exactly is conscience, and is there a difference in having a "Christian" conscience?

This chapter will explore the role of conscience in the moral life. By using concrete situations we will see how an understanding of conscience, the resources that assist it, and the responsibilities for the formation of conscience affect one's moral decisions. A process for making moral decisions will be introduced. The consequences of decisions are part of the moral responsibility each person carries as a member of the human family.

Conscience: Role and Function

Debra and James demonstrate the activity of conscience. Both "know" the right and wrong thing to do, the attitudes and dispositions of heart that are harmonious with their being. Debra knew she had done wrong, which created disharmony within herself and with others; James knew he wanted to help his parents and that he should offer help. Conscience is a type of knowledge that reveals what is right and what is wrong. It is a moral censor within the self that can be brilliant or dull, depending upon the openness and awareness one has of one's conscience and how well one has informed or sharpened the censor's sensors.

Inner Resources Assisting Conscience

Conscience operates with an inner knowledge that is not purely intellectual knowledge of facts, principles, or dictums. It is not a "voice" that whispers what is to be done, but it does communicate that through inner awareness. It is not a law, but it holds us to its demands and to accountability once certainty of conscience is reached. Conscience is the ability to marshal all we need to make a decision about what is morally right or wrong in a specific situation or in more general circumstances. Conscience employs all resources within a person to arrive at a decision. Such resources include one's faith, intellectual faculties of knowledge, memory and judgment, intuition, feelings, and body reactions ("gut" feelings). These resources help a person see the total picture and are valuable helps in revealing the moral route to be followed.

Inner resources from which the conscience draws its knowledge are shaped by many factors such as religion, experiences, relationships, needs and desires, education, age, and physical condition. A child has few experiences compared to an eighty-year-old man who has a lifetime of experiences that provide a rich fountain of wisdom from which he can draw to make moral decisions. The child is dependent on elders for advice and direction. *Age* and *experience* are resources that yield insights about people, situations, and the self that cannot be ignored by the conscience. *Intimate relationships* shape one's knowledge of people because they teach one about the needs and preferences of the other. Sometimes these are so necessary that honoring them is crucial to the physical and psychological health of the loved one; to ignore them is to risk illness and maybe death, the person's happiness and well-being. Only by having a level of intimacy with another does one gain this kind of personal knowledge that must be brought to bear in decisions of conscience.

Education is an inner resource for conscience. Religious education supplies us with the important knowledge of church teachings and traditions. The Ten Commandments, the commandments of love, and the teachings of the church on pertinent issues are invaluable resources when one is struggling to make a moral decision. Knowing where the church stands on medical issues, questions of life and death, labor and management issues, questions of the economy, immigrants, race relations, and political issues give the decision maker some helpful moral guidance. Clergy and pastoral-care givers should have extensive knowledge of church teaching and can be resources to those who have questions about church teachings or about moral dilemmas.

Education carries with it personal responsibility. David, a pharmacist, knows the effects of medication on heart patients while Sally, who has been buying a mix of over-the-counter drugs for her elderly father, who has a heart problem, does not fully understand how the mix might affect her father. David is "conscience bound" to use and share the knowledge he has; Sally does not have knowledge of pharmaceuticals, but she is "conscience bound" to care for her father. In terms of morality, a mistake by David in filling prescriptions is more serious than for Sally, for she lacks education and knowledge about the subject. Education continues to be a responsibility because new information is made available, and health professionals must keep abreast if they are to give others competent service. A doctor who does not know the latest developments in medicine and surgery could give less than adequate care to patients. Teachers must continue to learn in order to pass on current knowledge to their students. Theologians who do not continue to study theology and theological investigations are less able to serve the church and the faith community well. Conscience uses education as a resource to make moral decisions. Facts, statistics, studies, even theories provide objective information for the conscience.

Intuition is another type of knowledge that can be based on objective information, but it involves subjective processes to reach a conclusion. While all people have intuitive knowledge, some people use it as their first line of internal information. Mothers and fathers often rely on their intuition to know the needs of their children. A good friend intuitively knows what a friend would want in a situation of stress. Counselors rely on intuition to ask questions and make statements that disclose what is not obvious to the client. Teachers intuitively know when it is time to move to a new topic; a priest can sense when someone is ready to confess; and a husband knows intuitively when his wife wants affection and lovemaking. Intuition is knowledge based on data that are almost imperceptible to the untrained eye or ear because they are based on fleeting impressions gathered from gestures, words, facial expressions, pauses, and absences. The intuitive person is able to gather these impressions, which converge in one moment of knowledge that informs the conscience.

Prayer is another vital resource to conscience. Through personal contact with God in prayer, one can see life and its questions through the eyes of faith. Contemplation, scriptural readings, the mysteries of the faith, spiritual reading, inspirational music, and observation of nature can be avenues to glimpsing the mind and heart of God. Prayer opens one to a transcendental dimension of reality that the various human disciplines of study, education, experience, and relationships cannot reveal. Prayer activates faith and awakens it as a resource for conscience. For example, after prayer Katy may find forgiveness is the right thing to give, something mere logic could not dictate. Ben's prayer moves him to spend the weekend with his two sons rather than spending it fishing with his buddies. By bringing moral concerns to prayer, a person balances personal and faith dimensions of life. Prayer helps one to set priorities and maintain order that are consistent with one's inner core of being as it shapes one's conscience. Age, experience, intimate relationships, education, intuition, and prayer are some of the many inner resources used by the conscience to make a moral decision.

Conscience involves the entire person working with all the resources available, to make a right moral judgment. We see this happen when Ken, a store manager, agonizes over a tough and complicated decision to fire an employee. He reflects, studies, consults, prays, feels agitated, and may even lose his appetite and some sleep over the decision. Finally, if he is attuned to all the data within himself and without, Ken will make a decision consistent with the message of his conscience, and he will be at peace knowing he did the best he could with the resources available to him at the time.

Not all decisions are as taxing as Ken's. Most often moral decisions are easy to make. When conscience can draw on early years of formation, it can operate out of good habits that we call virtues. It is then second nature to "know" that certain things are morally wrong, and a decision to tell the truth or tell a lie can be made almost instantly. That is not to say a person will always follow the directives of conscience. All too often we attend to other messages and disobey our conscience, which directs us to the good, true, and right. In those cases we commit sin.

Vatican II and Conscience

The bishops of Vatican II define conscience as an internal law that binds a person to obedience. To obey the summons of conscience is to further the integration of the self to grow in consistency with what is believed at the core of the person. To disobey the internal law of conscience is to fracture the self at its very core. In disobedience to conscience, the self acts inconsistently with its own desires, wants, spiritual beliefs, and sense of right order:

> In the depth of his conscience, man detects a law which he does not impose upon himself, but which holds him to obedience. Always summoning him to love good and avoid evil, the voice of conscience can when necessary speak to his heart more specifically: do this, shun that. For man has in his heart a law written by God. To obey it is the very dignity of man; according to it he will be judged. Conscience is the most secret core and sanctuary of a man. (*Gaudium et Spes* 16)

In describing conscience as "the most secret core and sanctuary" of a person, the council bishops are saying conscience is personal and known chiefly by the person. It is personal because it is formed through each person's faith, family experiences, environment, education, social surroundings, personality, and all those other factors that influence the formation of conscience. Conscience is formed in ways that make it completely unique to the individual. In the end, no one person's conscience can substitute for another's because it is the individual who must make a decision in the depths of personal conscience at a given time. "Conscience is the *only* witness, since what takes place in the heart of the person is hidden from the eyes of everyone outside" (*Veritatis Splendor* 57).

If conscience is to operate at all, it must do so freely from one's own center of moral awareness. Decisions must be chosen in freedom without pressure. When personal freedom is lacking, people operate in blind obedience or in conformity to some strong authority figure, regarding what is thought to be good. In the same way, they can also be pressured or manipulated to take part in what is manifestly evil. Hence, the importance of deepening a free and personal response to conscience.[1] Freedom of conscience is also important because all decisions of conscience shape the self. By exercising conscience one grows as a person and comes to know oneself.

In 1993, Pope John Paul II issued an encyclical on the church's moral teachings, *Veritatis Splendor.* The pope is precise about the role of conscience: "Conscience is a moral judgment about man and his actions, a judgment either of acquittal or of condemnation, according as human acts are in conformity or not with the law of God written on the heart" (59). Conscience is a practical judgment that tells a person what to do or not do. Besides a judgment, conscience "formulates moral obligation in the light of the natural law: it is the obligation to do what the individual, through the workings of his conscience, knows to be a good he is called to do here and now" (59). Since all people know the natural law, the pope argues this is a universal and objective norm of morality. Conscience does not establish this law but rather bears witness to the natural law and its universal authority.

Conscience has a broader dimension than the personal one because it contains elements shared by most human beings. The social dimension of conscience reflects the values of a group, a city, a nation, or a country. A nation can realize as a whole that its government, even when endorsed by the people, has done wrong. This is true today of the German people, who regret the wrong done in exterminating the Jews during the Holocaust. The conscience of the United States acknowledges the immoral practices of slavery and racism. Conscience and some basic human values that undergird conscience seem to be knit in the sinew and bones of all people. Some common basic values include preservation of life, protection of the weak, truth telling, and honesty.

John Mahoney summarizes the work of conscience, including the various resources that operate in a decision:

> But just as we have a grasp of the rules of grammar, so we have
> a habitual grasp of the basic rules of morality. And conscience

"in the strict sense" is the action of applying such knowledge to our past or contemplated actions. The action of conscience, then, is no more and no less than an ordinary act of human reason applying the various principles of morality to individual situations.[2]

If conscience is an "ordinary act of human reason," then all people would have an inner knowledge of right and wrong such as the natural law and the Ten Commandments embody. Moral mandates such as these are "known" by all people simply because we share a common humanity, regardless of our experiences and environment. Based on this, it could be said everyone has a conscience and knows what is right and wrong, save those with warped and defective personalities. If everyone has a conscience of some type, is there anything unique about a Christian conscience?

Nature of Christian Conscience

A Christian conscience is first of all consistent with human nature. Christianity above all shows disciples how to live a fully human life, for only then is it a Christian life. Jesus showed us how to live as human beings — he was *fully human*. Jesus modeled the Christian way to be human, which at times goes against the current of cultural and popular opinion. A Christian conscience is based on the values and outlook of Jesus toward the world, society, relationships, work, and faith. All of life comes within the parameters of Christian conscience because all of life can be seen through the eyes of Jesus, and his teachings can be applied to many situations of life. The church provides help in applying Jesus' teachings through its moral norms, directives, pastoral letters, and encyclicals. Bishops and pastoral ministers are there to guide us in decisions of conscience. The teachings of the magisterium guide the faith community not only in making moral decisions but also in forming consciences because the teachings point the direction to truth, justice, goodness, and love. Pope John Paul II has reminded Christians of the great help the church and its magisterium provide in the formation of conscience:

As the Council affirms: "In forming their consciences the Christian faithful must give careful attention to the sacred and certain teaching of the Church. For the Catholic Church is by the will of Christ the teacher of truth. Her charge is to announce and teach authentically that truth which is Christ, and at the same time with her authority to declare and confirm the principles of the moral order which derive from human nature itself." (*Evangelium Vitae* 84, quoting *Dignitatis Humanae* 14)

Good teachings educate consciences to the mind and heart of Jesus. The role of the magisterium is to provide good teaching; but it is also the duty of the magisterium to inspire conscience, not to substitute for it.[3]

Primacy of Conscience and Erroneous Conscience

When a moral decision is made, conscience is the final arbiter of what is right. A long-held tradition of the church is that "conscience is primary." This means conscience holds the primary place and responsibility for making moral decisions. In the mind of St. Thomas Aquinas and in the tradition of the church, conscience is the immediate perceiver of God's will and is *to be followed always, in every circumstance:* "Conscience obliges in the sense that whoever acts against his conscience has the will to sin. Consequently, if someone believes that by not fornicating he commits a mortal sin, he chooses to commit a mortal sin by not committing the act. And therefore he does sin mortally."[4] Aquinas clearly articulates the importance of following one's conscience. Theologian Josef Rudin relates the teaching of Aquinas to one's relationship to the magisterium and its teaching authority. "Anyone upon whom the ecclesiastical authority, in ignorance of the true facts, imposes a demand that offends against his clear conscience, should perish in excommunication rather than violate his conscience."[5]

Once all authorities, internal and external, have been consulted, reflection and prayer can help one reach a decision. That decision is to be freely made in conscience by the discerner. In the end, the decision of conscience is primary, and conscience must be followed. The strong endorsement of conscience as the primary place for moral decisions has been upheld in the tradition of the church. Cardinal John Henry Newman, who is a recognized church leader, often wrote in defense of the primacy of conscience:

> [W]hen I speak of conscience, I mean conscience truly so-called. ...If in a particular case it is to be taken as a sacred and sovereign monitor, its dictates, in order to prevail against the voice of the Pope, must follow upon serious thought, prayer, and all available means of arriving at a right judgment on the matter in question.[6]

The pope and bishops have referred to the tradition of primacy of conscience in their teachings since Vatican II. In *Humanae Vitae*, Paul VI wrote that "a right conscience is the true interpreter of the objective moral order instituted by God" (10). In subsequent commentaries on *Humanae Vitae* the hierarchy has stated that "we recognize the role of conscience as a 'practical dictate,' not a teacher of doctrine."[7]

As stated above, conscience is *to be followed always, in every circumstance,* even when it is in error. Conscience can be in error because it is not perfect. Error is less likely when a careful decision-making process has been followed, but even with this, human beings can make mistakes of judgment. Some likely reasons for errors are haste, lack of knowledge, "inculpable ignorance," immaturity, personal pressures, and dysfunctional personality. Objective criteria can seldom be remembered when one is in haste and certainly when there is no time to consult or to study the issue. Haste may preclude knowledge. However, when a judgment is made contrary to objective criteria of morality and there is no source of knowledge available, this is called "inculpable ignorance." There is no subjective fault because no information was available, although there is objective error.

In the cases cited above, the error concerns objective knowledge of right and wrong, not the internal decision of right and wrong. If a person believes in conscience that something is right, then that must be followed even when objectively it is considered to be morally wrong and a mortal sin. For example, a person believing in conscience that to tell a lie in a certain situation is the morally right thing would be doing the morally right thing if she or he lied, but objectively speaking the person would be working with an erroneous conscience.

Still other sources of error can be immaturity, pressure or stress, illness, and a dysfunctional personality. Each of these could be seen as forms of "inculpable ignorance." A person might be incapable of a more mature judgment because of age, physical inability to think clearly and well, lack of psychological maturity, or psychological problems. Each of these hampers our awareness of objective truth and the application of moral principles, and judgment is impaired.

In the case of psychological factors, some find it extremely difficult to be open to church authority because of their past negative experiences with parental authority figures. They are incapable of being open to any authority for advice, information, and guidance. Resentment of persons or institutions that have authority stands in the way of hearing the wisdom and moral insight available. Until a position of psychological freedom has been reached, they are not able to hear the values and freedom of Jesus' message. Human beings hear Jesus' voice only imperfectly, but as Vatican II states, "Conscience *frequently errs from invincible ignorance* without losing its dignity" (*Gaudium et Spes* 16).

Errors in conscience can arise from culpable ignorance. "Culpable ignorance" describes the attitude of one who chooses not to be informed on moral issues. Information and guidance are available, but the person rejects these. Culpable ignorance pertains to those who purposely disregard church teaching, resist any advice and offers of help, and ignore opportunities for religious education. Moral wrong is present because the decisions are made for self-centered reasons that are not based on the stance of the church. The teachings of Jesus are overlooked, if not scorned, especially as they are applied through the church's magisterium. Here a lack of openness to moral teachings and the work of the Spirit is evident, and a callous rejection of truth indicates a choice for sin.

Disciples of Jesus are called to be informed and to learn about the moral teachings of Jesus and about the church that interprets and applies them. Reasonable efforts must be made to become knowledgeable. Unreasonable efforts can lead to scrupulosity, which is not a position that is morally sound. Laxity, in contrast, takes a *laissez-faire* attitude that is also not morally sound. The formation of conscience is a moral responsibility carried by each disciple.

Formation of Mature Conscience

The formation of a Christian conscience is a lifetime task. It begins in the faith of parents who impart the values and practices of the faith to their infant children. While a child cannot "know" right from wrong until it is taught, the child can learn Christian values and incorporate them in time as his or her own. Eventually a child learns what is right.

The Role of Examples

Formation of conscience is more often done by example than by words. Psychologists know human beings learn more from people whom they love and who love them than from abstract teaching. Children at play can be seen imitating their parents, using the very

words, actions, and gestures their parents use. Children are most
strongly formed by their primary caregivers, who usually are parents, but other significant relationships also influence the formation
of a person and of conscience. The axioms "Tell me who your friends
are and I will tell you who you are" and "Birds of a feather flock together" hold true for the formation of conscience. We are shaped by
significant relationships within our families, by our friends, neighbors, and colleagues. Paul VI, in his encyclical *Evangelii Nuntiandi*
recognized the power of relationships and good teachers when he
spoke of the importance of witness: "Modern man listens more will-
ingly to witnesses than to teachers, and if he does listen to teachers, it
is because they are witnesses" (41).[8] A Christian conscience is most
truly formed and educated by the witness of good Christians, particularly those with whom a person has a close relationship of love.
This anecdote illustrates the power of one person:

> Fifty years ago a Johns Hopkins professor gave a group of grad-
> uate students this assignment: go to the slums, take 220 boys,
> investigate their backgrounds and environment, and then pre-
> dict their chances for the future. The students concluded that
> 90 percent of the boys would spend some time in jail.
>
> Twenty-five years later another group of graduate students
> was given the job of testing the prediction. They found that
> only four of the group had ever been sent to jail.
>
> How could this be, as these men had lived in a breeding place
> for crime? The researchers were continually told: "Well, there
> was this teacher...." In pressing further they found that in 75
> percent of the cases it was the same woman. The researchers
> found her living in a home for retired teachers and asked her
> how she exerted this remarkable influence. She couldn't say,
> except to comment: "I loved those boys...."

The formation of a Christian conscience is not solely dependent
on the efforts of others such as parents and teachers and friends. It is
primarily the work of the individual and is finally the person's own
responsibility. While commenting on human development, Paul VI
wrote words that can equally apply to the formation of conscience:
"And man is only truly man in as far as, master of his own acts and
judge of their worth, *he is author of his own advancement*, in keeping with nature which was given to him by his Creator and whose
possibilities and exigencies he himself freely assumes" (*Populorum
Progressio* 34).[9]

I am responsible for choosing those people and relationships that will be consistent with the faith, values, and dreams I hold important. All of us can choose to have those persons in our lives who affirm our values and beliefs. While it is true that no one can control all people entering one's life, one can choose significant relationships that will witness to what is of value.

Liturgy and Imagination

> Every man has the duty, and therefore the right, to seek truth in matters religious, in order that he may with prudence form for himself right and true judgments of conscience, with the use of all suitable means.   — *Dignitatis Humanae* 3

The formation of conscience is ongoing throughout one's life. It can grow just as one's perspective on all of life matures; it can develop as one's spirituality grows. The more one desires to take on the mind and heart of Jesus, the more one's Christian conscience can mature. Such development requires an openness to the spiritual life through prayer and worship. The liturgy is a powerful means of moral education through the sacraments and the Liturgies of the Word and the Eucharist. Through symbol and ritual, deeper levels of the self are touched. Human longings, desires, and spiritual needs find expression in good liturgy. Liturgy also forms the "inner core and depths" of a person, which the bishops call conscience.

Liturgy frees the imagination to hear the Word of God anew. When the senses of hearing, smell, sight, and touch are awakened, the imagination can form new images evoked by the scriptures and the liturgies. Sign and symbol speak to the deepest levels of the self and suggest new possibilities of the Kingdom in this day, bringing those possibilities from the internal level to external reality. At the internal level, conscience is educated through the imagination formed by the Word of God. Reading the scriptures can open the door of one's mind to new insights of how God works with people. Through the scriptures we can image a more just world, more loving relationships, forgiveness of those who have offended us, and the efforts needed to help those in need. One could say that the Kingdom of God is known first of all through the imagination. Here one envisions how Jesus perceives reality, and here Christian conscience is solidified.

Living a life of love with significant relationships to which one is faithful can teach one the ways of love and so educate one's conscience. After a couple has been married for a couple of years, they can relate the many things they have learned about each other and about ways to love each other better. With the coming of children, new dimensions of love are born that also educate conscience. Faithful love turns lovers outward and is not turned in on the couple. Love can impel one to seek justice for all people. Participation in politics and government, working with the poor and disenfranchised, educates one's conscience to aspects of the gospel teachings in ways reading or hearing the text cannot do. Participation and active involvement are educators of conscience. Study and course work to learn more about scripture and the church's teaching are others ways of educating one's conscience. Each of these means to form one's conscience is the personal responsibility of each believer. However, that responsibility is shared with members of the faith community who are there to assist members of the community and by leaders of the faith community who maintain the traditions of the community through moral teachings made available to all members.

Moral Decision Making: Communal and Faith Dimensions

At the beginning of this chapter, the cases of Winnie, Debra, and James were presented. Each had made a decision following their own process. We can now look at the moral decision-making process itself in the light of Vatican II's understanding of conscience, the unique character of Christian conscience, the resources available to conscience, and the moral situation at hand. An examination of the process can perhaps best be undertaken through situations requiring a moral decision. We shall examine the moral dilemmas of a young woman, a businessman, and a middle-aged woman and use the communal and faith dimensions of religion as aids to the conscience in making a moral decision.

Each of the cases highlights difficult decisions that must be made. The decisions are not simply legal, financial, or medical matters but also involve moral judgments. Relationships, care for others, responsibilities, obedience to a law, and scandal are moral considerations that must be addressed. What is the best way to take moral matters into the decision-making process? The following might be a framework that can assist a person who is making a moral decision.

Case 1: Jessie and Sally

Jessie and Sally were best friends throughout their school years.
They shared everything, went on vacations with each other's
families, and always went to school functions together. There
were times when Jessie's mother was sure Bell Telephone re-
mained in business because the girls called each other so often.
During their senior year of high school, Mrs. Thomson noticed
that Jessie, her daughter, was not calling Sally as often and
Sally came over infrequently. When Mrs. Thomson asked about
Sally, Jessie replied that Sally had changed in recent months,
was withdrawn and often irritable. Jessie seemed hesitant to
talk about the reason for the change in Sally's personality, and
Mrs. Thomson wondered if Sally was on drugs. Later that
evening she shared her suspicion with Jessie. Early that semester
Jessie had suspected the same and had confronted Sally, who
had become very defensive. Then the fact that Sally was often
talking to Mr. Arens made Jessie wonder if their English teacher
was not supplying Sally with drugs. He was married and had
three children. "Why didn't you mention this to me?" "Because
I was not sure if drugs were the problem. If I have no proof
and only my suspicions it wouldn't be right to say anything
that could hurt Sally and Mr. Arens." *What is the morally right
thing for Jessie and her mother to do?*

Case 2: Nick

Nick works as a supervisor for a construction company. His
careful work has earned him the trust of his employers as well
as the respect of co-workers. Recently there was a change in
ownership. Nick retained his post, but he began to notice some
managerial changes that involved materials. The new owners
wanted to see more profit, so they ordered the construction
materials from a different supplier. Nick soon realized the product may have appeared suitable to the untrained eye, but he
knew the materials were inferior and would not last. While
they would not cause major problems in the construction, Nick
knew customers were not getting their money's worth — they
were being cheated. At a meeting with his new boss, Nick tact-
fully spoke about the inferior quality of the materials being
used. Nick was told he could find a new job if he did not like

the new way of doing things. "We're here to make money and people know that when they come to us." If Nick says nothing, his workers will think this type of construction is suitable. They will condone the situation because Nick does. *Should Nick at age fifty quit his job?* At his age, Nick knows it will be difficult to land another supervisory position, and with two kids in college, he really needs the income.

Case 3: Alice and Mother

Alice had to take her elderly mother to a nursing home following a long period of illness and hospitalization. Her mother suffers from several complicating problems, chief of which is heart disease. Balancing the various medications is a tricky thing because one can trigger reactions from the others. Last night Alice received a call that her mother had had a stroke that left her right side paralyzed and had affected her mother's breathing and other bodily functions. There seems to be little chance of recovery. The doctors have had to take her mother off medications, which makes the situation precarious, but they most fear another stroke or heart failure. Alice is facing a decision of DNR — "Do Not Resuscitate" — should another crisis arise. *What are the moral options available to Alice? As a woman who loves her mother, what is the loving thing to do?*

The Process of Moral Decision Making

The process begins with a state of mind that is open to the Spirit as ways of truth, love, and justice emerge. The disciple enters this process in a spirit of faith that God is present and will make known the right route to follow. God can speak through any of the means human beings use to reach wisdom.

Three Font Principle: Intention, Circumstances, Act

The moral tradition of the church provides us with a balanced means to analyze the human acts. To determine the morality of a human act, tradition considers three factors: the act itself, its circumstances, and the intention of the actor. This has been called

the three font principle. All acts are cast in a context with varying circumstances that color them. The act of stealing is a morally
wrong act when taken objectively, but when stealing is cast in the
context of Oliver Twist, who was trained as a boy to become an ex-
pert pick-pocket, the act takes on a different meaning. For Oliver
Twist being an accomplished thief was good. The training to steal,
the age of the stealer, his hunger and poverty, fear of punishment
and loss of a home — all these affected the moral nature of Oliver
Twist's act.

With the renewal in moral theology, the three font principle
has been retrieved to serve a person-centered morality. Prior to
Vatican II, Scholasticism and casuistry refined definitions of moral
actions neatly and precisely. Little attention was given to intention
and circumstances while primary attention was given to determining
the nature of the act based on moral norms. In a person-centered
morality, the traditional three font principle of act, circumstance,
and intention can be used to analyze moral acts. However, attention must be given to balancing the three terms in such a way that
no one element receives primary attention and all three are given due
importance. Without this balance, aberrations of morality such as
relativism, emotivism, and subjectivism could emerge.[10] With such a
balance, a human act can be fully understood as present in a person's
life, coming from the "stuff" of that person's life, yet also standing in the arena of the community that established objective norms
about good and evil. Once the complete picture is viewed, reason and
will can be used to make moral decisions compatible with Christian
discipleship.

Important to the decision-making process is a spirit of prayer and
trust. A quiet place, ample time, and a relaxed environment will help
discerners to "hear" the Word of God revealed and enable them to
make a free decision that is truly their own. A pad of paper and
a pencil may be helpful tools. Do a practice run by choosing to
make a moral decision for one of the cases cited above, using the
framework below.

1. *Be clear about what must be decided.*

   • In one sentence, state what must be decided.

   • List the issues that pertain to the situation and rank them.

   • List all questions that come to mind pertaining to the
     issue.

2. *Consider religious beliefs pertaining to the situation.*

- List all questions, thoughts, and material that have a religious bearing on the issue.

- In your mind, how would Jesus look at the situation?

- What would Jesus do as a friend and an observer of the Law?

- Consider the religious faith of the discerner. Would religious faith require the person to do something?

- Does the church offer any specific guidance through its teachings on this matter?

- If you do not know what your faith offers on the matter, it may help to talk with a priest or pastoral minister about the situation. Christian faith puts life's dilemmas into focus by seeing them through the eyes of Jesus and from a transcendental perspective. How much will this situation matter in eternity? One's spiritual outlook will color how one listens to all input on the situation.

3. *Ask honest questions; seek reliable sources for answers.*

- Write down any questions you are afraid of asking someone.

- About which questions do you have the strongest feelings?

- What are the feelings emerging with the decision?

- Are your feelings clouding your view of things so that you are biased rather than open-minded about the possibilities?

- Is there a fair, clearheaded, caring person to whom you can speak about your concerns?

- Is there a professional person who has studied and knows about the matters pertaining to the case?

- Are there some books, videos, or other reliable sources of information you can use to learn more about the situation?

4. *Summarize the information and feelings; dialogue and reflect.*

- List in two columns the factual information learned and your feelings.

- Mark those that "feel right." Circle those that are disturbing.

- Dialogue with a trusted and wise person about the information and about your feelings. What is disturbing about some options? Are the "feel right" options easy answers that will be comfortable but not give the best long-term response? What is most consistent with your religious faith?

- Take time to reflect on new information you learned about yourself during this step of the process.

5. *Pray, Test, and Decide.*

- Formulate a decision.

- Could this decision be justly and lovingly applied to every human being in the same situation?

- Are you considering only your wants and desires or are you considering the common good?

- Pray with an open mind and heart about the formulated decision. What are Jesus' words to you?

- What feelings emerge from your decision and your prayer?

- Do you have feelings of love, joy, and peace and an attitude of patience, kindness, goodness, faithfulness, gentleness, and self-control?

- If these feelings and attitudes persist, then you can surmise your decision is consistent with your conscience and is a right decision.

- If there are troubling and uneasy feelings and thoughts about the decision, reformulate the answer and try to arrive at a new one. If these feelings and thoughts persist, it may be necessary to explore steps 1, 2, and 3 again.

Step 3 is a difficult one for some people. When a moral problem exists, it is often a dilemma because of emotional ties between the participants. As friends, Jessie and Sally are bound by innumerable ties formed during years of friendship. Jessie's loyalty overrides her ability to seek the best for her friend and Mr. Arens. Nick has a good working relationship based on trust between himself and those under him. He may not be able to see the perspective of his new boss, and he may be overly concerned about his fellow workers. Perhaps he underestimates his ability to find a new job. Alice has a daughter's deep love for her mother, which can hamper her ability to make life and death decisions for her. Emotional ties make it very difficult to take an objective stand and see the most obvious answers. It is difficult, if not impossible at times, for the people most involved in the moral dilemma to make good judgments because of their emotional bias. However, that does not excuse them from the moral responsibility they face in conscience when a decision must be made.

The person who is able to have a balanced view of the situation can answer questions honestly and is not afraid of the hard questions. For others who seem entangled with some emotional or factual bias, a loving friend, counselor, or pastoral-care giver can help sort out the "objective facts" from the "emotional facts." This helper can assist the person to find an answer that balances factual data with emotional leanings. One may need to consult trained professionals for answers to questions beyond the competency of people involved. This refers to questions involving medical procedures and legal obligations. Getting input from more than one professional is common practice and will assure the person that all has been done to arrive at a right decision. This pertains to Jessie's dilemmas and the legal implications regarding illegal use of drugs, and to the medical questions of Alice regarding her mother.

In step 4, the discerner is asked to summarize what has been learned from reflection and from consultation. It is helpful at this point to list the important bits of data and the significant feelings involved in the decision. The lists of data and feelings will reveal consistencies and inconsistencies. A "factually, objectively right" decision that makes good common sense may be obvious, but if the person does not "feel right" about it, more dialogue and reflection are needed. Sometimes a person has not fully understood the situation and the options. More dialogue can clarify this. "Feeling right" can come with time and more information. When decisions are made without sufficient time for reflection, people can feel "ramrodded" into a decision and consequently feel it is not their own decision. They do not own it even though they made it. This would be the case if Alice was given one hour to decide about her mother's situation. Sometimes a day, a week, or longer is needed until a right and moral answer can be given. There are times, however, when time is not available, and a decision must be made with the best resources available. In retrospect the person may realize it was not the right decision but can always rest assured it was the best decision given the constraints of the situation.

The final step is to pray, test, and decide. Reflection will often naturally lead to prayer for the person of faith. Petitions could include asking for light to see the way to be followed, insight into the faith dimension of the situation, the views of the other, or strength and courage to make a good decision and the ability to live by it. Prayer will help one recall God's presence. God is present at all times but especially in those situations that push us to our limits such as stress, decision making, and pain. Grace is given to enable human beings to achieve the most satisfying and right moral decisions — we are never alone or unable to do what is required because we have God's help.

Testing the Moral Decision

There are several ways one can test the rightness or wrongness of a moral decision. The first way tests internal responses to the decision. St. Paul used certain feelings and attitudes as guides to recognize the work of the Spirit. "But the fruit of the Spirit is love, joy, peace, patience, kindness, goodness, faithfulness, gentleness, self-control; against such there is no law" (Gal. 6:22). When these Christian attitudes, feelings, and behaviors are present, then one can be certain that the decision is a right moral decision.

A second test of a right moral decision is the inclusion of both the needs of the individual person and the needs of the community. Christians take a communal perspective on the moral good, so all personal goods are not solely for the individual but serve the good of all. Moral decisions take into consideration the community of faith through the teachings of the magisterium on moral matters. Is this decision consistent with the teachings and beliefs of the church?

Philosopher Immanuel Kant's "categorical imperative" is also helpful as an intellectual test of right thinking. Once a tentative decision is made, test it by applying it to every person in the same situation. Would it serve each one's good? Would it stand the test of universalizability? Could the answer be applied universally to everyone? The test of "universalizability" eliminates self-serving answers and brings the common good into focus.

Sometimes there may be a conflict between the individual good and the common good. Pope John Paul II said in 1981 that individual good is subordinate to the common good, which is to be preferred. "The right to private property is subordinated to the right to common use, to the fact that goods are meant for everyone" (*Laborem Exercens* 14). In 1987, the pope reiterated his position: "It is necessary to state once more the characteristic principle of Christian social doctrine: the goods of this world are *originally meant for all*. The right to private property is *valid and necessary*, but it does not nullify the value of this principle" (*Sollicitudo Rei Socialis* 42).[11]

A right moral decision will satisfy one's conscience. The decision may be difficult, even painful, but if it is the right one, eventually peace, love, and joy will ensue. A right decision will fulfill the good of the individual and the common good.

Consequences of Actions

Moral decisions will lead to attitudes, behaviors, and actions. Some of these can be foreseen during the decision-making process; others may not have been evident; and still others may emerge in time. These could not have been foreseen. Debra did not foresee that her friend would spread a rumor about her mother-in-law. Jessie did not see that her silence in dealing with Sally may have allowed her friend to become more seriously addicted to drugs and in debt to her English teacher. We are morally responsible for all consequences we can foresee happening; however, we cannot avoid doing the right simply because some consequences are unpleasant, uncomfortable, or awkward. This would be consequentialism. The "right" must be set against a larger backdrop that includes the many factors beside consequences that enter into a moral decision.

A final test of a right moral decision does include consequences. Can I live with both the positive and negative effects of my decision? On the one hand, this might mean Nick will be fired and out of work, that when Alice decides on DNR she will lose her mother within a week, that Jessie will lose Sally as a friend and Mr. Arens will be arrested for peddling drugs. If there is uncertainty about a decision that will have drastic consequences, time and consultation are important until certainty of conviction can be reached. On the other hand, Nick finally might have the opportunity to start his own construction company; Sally will get help for depression, which Mr. Arens recognized as her problem; and Alice's mother could die before Alice has to make a decision about DNR. Consequences cannot always be predicted. Although we cannot foresee all of the consequences of a moral decision, *we are morally responsible for those actions that cause unjustified harm, distress, anxiety, and hurt to anyone.* This must be considered in the decision-making process.

Some would say, "This is too much! How can I possibly handle all the tension of the decision and the consequences, seen and unseen?" The escapist would want to avoid making any decisions and so avoid unpleasant consequences. The disciple, with God's help, must be decisive and trust the self to make good moral decisions, even when these are difficult. Jessie must risk losing the friendship of Sally; Nick may suffer financial loss; Alice may lose her mother in death. Christians are called to follow Christ and his life in the world, an arduous discipleship that calls for confrontation, alienation at times, and courage. There are times when we regret a decision, but that does not justify making no decision when one is required. We must live in the present and work with the Spirit present in the world we encounter here and now. The disciple of Jesus can do no other than make a moral response in the present. If justice is to grow, then the followers of Jesus must confront the structures of injustice operating now; if love is to grow, then loving actions must be done now; if peace is to flourish, then ways of peace rather than violent ways must be lived now. To not act and make a moral decision now is to allow what is wrong or evil to continue, and in some sense to condone it by inaction. Moral decisiveness promotes moral maturity, for it is in the process of decision making and in dealing with the consequences of our decisions that we grow.

Conclusion

Winnie the Pooh, Debra, and James all made decisions: Winnie stole honey out of instinct because he did not have human moral capabilities; Debra made a decision out of psychological pressure, in haste and impulsively; James made a decision out of love and concern. The most human decision was made by James, who used his conscience to follow values of love, care, concern, and responsibility. He reflected on his decision and knew it was the right one. Reason, values, and reflection are human capabilities. When moral decisions are made carefully, they reflect the values of the person and promote maturity. If one takes time for prayer and reflection, one can bring Christian perspectives to bear and see the situation through the eyes of Jesus. Time allows one to engage the full range of human capabilities to arrive at a decision and permits one to use reason and faith. To make a decision is to take a stand for Christian values and principles, a decision that promotes moral maturity. Besides helping persons like Debra, James, Jessie, Nick, and Alice to grow, a good moral decision helps others in the community. A right moral decision for an individual is a right moral decision for the community.

Notes

1. George V. Lobo, S.J., *Guide to Christian Living* (Westminster, Md.: Christian Classics, 1984), 289.

2. John Mahoney, *The Making of Moral Theology* (Oxford: Clarendon Press, 1987), 188.

3. Lobo, *Guide*, 293.

4. Thomas Aquinas, *Summa Theologiae*, Ia-Ilae, q. 19, art. 5.

5. The reference is to IV Sent., disp. 38, q. II, art. 4.

6. Cardinal Newman, "A Letter to the Duke of Norfolk," quoted in National Conference of Catholic Bishops, *Human Life in Our Day* (Boston: Daughters of St. Paul, 1968), 40.

7. National Conference of Catholic Bishops, *Human Life*, 14.

8. Ibid., 14.

9. Pope Paul VI, address to the members of the Consilium de Laicis, October 2, 1974, in *AAS* 66 (1974): 568.

10. Relativism is the view that ethical truths depend on the individuals and groups holding them rather than on external criteria such as revealed truths found in Christianity, natural law, or some other unchanging source of truth. Emotivism is the belief that moral truths are derived from one's emotions or feelings, likes and dislikes, which originate in conditioning. Subjectivism depends on the person, his or her personal views and opinions, for moral truth. Objective sources of truth stand in opposition to this view, which encompasses relativism and emotivism.

11. See also *Gaudium et Spes* 69; *Populorum Progressio* 22; *Lumen Gentium* 90; Thomas Aquinas, *Summa Theologiae*, II–IIe, q. 66, art. 2.

Chapter 8

FOUNDATIONS AND LESSONS: THEN AND NOW

The morning paper and the TV news anchor bring us "up to speed" with the breaking news events of the country and the world. Election results, medical breakthroughs, political and military tensions, catastrophic accidents, and Wall Street — all find a spot in the news. We get a glimpse of history in the making as we begin to make our own life history for the day. Each of the current events is built on a history of events in the past, such as Mideast tensions that have existed for decades or the platform of a political party that was established in past centuries. In one way, we could say history structures the present, and we apply its lessons to situations at hand. In another way, everything is new, and today's events add another page to history, which is being written even now.

Having examined important facets of Christian morality, we can now ask, What does all of this mean? How do the moral tradition of the past and its history factor into our present time, the new day before us? This chapter will look at the meaning of moral traditions across time. From this perspective we may be able to see just how meaningful and life-giving these traditions were for men and women over the centuries. We may also be able to discover ways in which the long held traditions of Christianity have elements that are ever-new and significant to present-day disciples. We will examine some contemporary moral challenges Christian disciples face to see if history can enlighten our search for meaning and guide us in addressing the challenges.

Contemporary Moral Challenges

Disciples today are challenged morally by many problems in society. We will examine three social tendencies that may find parallels in our exploration into historical study: individualism, materialism, and secularism.

Life in a First World country such as the United States, Canada, or certain nations in Europe economically is a level above the squalor of countries in the Southern Hemisphere. We can usually count on having food, shelter, electricity, running water, and educational opportunities that many people in Third World countries do not have. We are convinced that hard work and perseverance usually will merit us a good living and property we can call our own. "We have earned what we own — it is ours. Anyone who does not work should not 'get.'" At times this is a prevalent attitude, one that protects our own interests, but it also tends to breed individualism and isolationism because the concern is primarily about us and not about others who are our neighbors. The Christian tradition is a communitarian one that seeks the common good for all people.

First World citizens enjoy the goods of the earth, goods often mined and drilled and raised in other countries of the world. As wealth increases, material goods are more accessible. The danger is that the availability of goods and the possession of ever-more things can make them an end in themselves. Materialism springs up when life is wrapped around things. Materialists are people who usually do not want for things and sometimes seem not to need people or even God. They have all they need in their property and possessions. When the possession of things becomes an end in itself, it can supplant spiritual needs. Can events of the past tell us anything about the issue of possessions and spiritual needs?

Another issue facing contemporary Christians is secularism. The "secular spirit" gained a strong foothold during the 1960s with its revolutionary spirit. Religious structures were rejected as meaningless and "out of touch." More often religion was treated with indifference or was taken out of the institutional setting. As the computer age developed, people looked to science and technology and not to faith for answers to life's questions. They found they did not have to be religious to lead a meaningful life. Is this indifference to religion a new problem, or did secularism penetrate religious communities in the past? Did they have to deal with conflicts between the secular and religious spheres of life?

Individualism, materialism, and secularism continue to confront the church as moral issues today. Can we find a precedent in the history of moral theology to see whether and how disciples from earlier generations dealt with similar questions in their societies? To answer the questions raised by each of these contemporary moral issues, we will use a contemporary lens, "a contemporary eye," to view the past and to examine the moral traditions and practices found in history that may instruct us today. To find answers to contemporary questions, we will explore the eras of Christian moral tradition beginning with the early years of the church.

History of the Development of the Moral Tradition

Each period of history is shaped by the social, political, and economic conditions of the world at the time. The first period of Christianity began with the life of Jesus and his followers, the apostles and early leaders of the church. This period of history was more fully discussed in chapter 2 and will be addressed again in chapter 9, when we study the Christocentric approach of Vatican II and its focus on a biblical basis for a renewal of moral theology. For now, we will recall that early disciples faced practical questions about how to live their baptismal commitment in a world that did not share their Christian beliefs. The first disciples of Jesus encountered a situation that had a striking similarity to our own: a diversity of religious beliefs in a secular world.

Apostolic and Patristic Eras

This first period, called the Apostolic and Patristic Eras, encompasses the early stages of the Christian community until about A.D. 400. Named after the apostles and early "Fathers" (holy men and scholars) of the church, this period focused on several concerns pertinent to the strengthening of the Christian community.

One concern was teaching and preaching the Word of God. The apostles traveled throughout the Mediterranean region and beyond preaching the Word they had heard and witnessed. Their early followers transcribed the preaching, and so began oral and written forms of the Christian tradition. The church leaders were preoccupied with transmitting the message of revelation faithfully to the new converts, who had practical questions regarding everyday moral dilemmas that arose from the society in which they lived. Questions about military service, adultery, the value of virginity, and the forgiveness of major sins were but a few of the concerns of early Christians.

Christianity had to be taught in the context of Greek and Roman philosophies that were prevalent in society at that time. Christians needed to differentiate their beliefs and moral standards from the Jewish religion, the Greek and Roman philosophies, and pagan religions. The scriptures were a prime source of knowledge for the early Christians regarding moral perspectives, but more specific applications of scriptural understandings were needed.

St. Paul provided this in letters to the various communities he established. Paul's views were shaped by his belief that Jesus' second coming would be soon, a belief that influenced his moral instruction. Paul wrote extensively on moral dilemmas facing his communities in Corinth and Rome. We can also find his straightforward opinions and views in letters to the Thessalonians, Hebrews, Philippians, and to Timothy and Philemon. Topics addressed by Paul include sexual ethics, communal life, labor and economics, interpersonal relationships, marriage and family life, conduct of priests, political leadership, and personal ethics. Regarding sexual conduct, Paul tells the Corinthians, "The body is not meant for immorality, but for the Lord, and the Lord for the body.... Do you not know that he who joins himself to a prostitute becomes one body with her?... But he who is united to the Lord becomes one spirit with him" (1 Cor. 6:15–16). To Titus, Paul writes that Christians are to be submissive to rulers and authorities, do honest work, speak evil of no one, avoid quarreling, be gentle, and show perfect courtesy toward all. In his letters, Paul brought clarity to specific moral questions through his directives regarding the moral life of a Christian. No moral or religious issue raised by his converts and disciples was overlooked by Paul, who based his knowledge both on the teachings of Jesus and on his own belief that the Kingdom of God would come soon.

Today we treasure the basic elements of the moral tradition that were hammered out in the first centuries of Christianity. Tensions, dilemmas, questions, and differences of culture brought early church leaders and scholars together for dialogue, study, and sometimes heated debate. What practices of the Jewish religion would be maintained in Christianity? If Jesus was fully divine, then was he truly human? What beliefs would a new member of the Christian community have to espouse? Some of these questions and dilemmas were influenced by pagan religions and pagan practices that competed for followers, by the persecution of believers, and by the Jewish religion. Some of the teachings of Jesus ran counter to the teachings and practices of these cultural and religious groups. Newly baptized Christians were in transition from one worldview of religion and morality to a new worldview of Christian belief and morality. While

Christian belief was strong, previous patterns of thought and behaviors, ingrained from childhood, were often stronger. Moreover, there were no officially established norms and practices in the first years of Christianity. These needed to be determined. The Church Fathers played a significant role in developing a body of moral practices.

Monasticism

Some of the early believers encountered the moral evils of society and fled to the desert to escape them. There arose monasteries of men and women who wanted to live only for God, free from sin. These early beginnings of the monastic movement, however, were not so much an escape from the evil of big cities as they were an effort by hermits and monks to confront the evil in their own hearts. In time, Christians hailed the desert and monastic recluses as the holy ones because of their penitential lifestyle. This qualified them to lead others to holiness through advice and spiritual guidance. St. Anthony, one of the early Desert Fathers, influenced many who sought to live the Christian moral life. Another significant figure in the monastic movement was St. Benedict, the father of Western monasticism. The Western church is indebted to him for the Rule of Benedict that later became the model for the rules of many monastic and religious orders and a foundation for Christian spirituality.

Another manifestation of this ascetic perspective was the *Didache* (ca. A.D. 75), which was a compilation of the moral teachings in the early years of the church. This text was written by pastors and monks who served the local church. It was organized according to the scheme of the Two Ways used by a Jewish ascetic group called the Essene community: the way of virtue leading to salvation and the way of evil leading to ruin. The *Didache* was not an academic work but rather was written to inspire the reader to conversion and to meet the concrete needs of the local church. It served a pastoral use rather than a doctrinal use. The *Didache* did not reflect the teachings and beliefs of all church leaders.

Contemporary Eye on the Past:
Secularism

We are faced with tensions between the secular world and the sacred today, but as the account of early Christianity reveals, this is not a new tension. Early followers of Christ knew firsthand the pressures between fidelity to their religious beliefs and practices and the philosophical and cultural influences of a pagan environment. These pioneering Christians used several means to deal with conflicts between the two realms of their lives and with secularism.

They turned to community leaders for advice and leadership. The Acts of the Apostles, the letters of Paul and Peter, and other early writings of church leaders reveal moral conflicts confronting the apostles and early church bishops. After many meetings — even councils — and dialogue, the leaders made decisions that guided the community. In some cases Christians were urged to avoid certain people who would have a negative influence on them; they were not to attend some gatherings, and in other cases they were to resist evil by actively speaking against it. Some Christians decided to flee the "world" because they believed the secular realm was fraught with evil. While monks who fled the world took an extreme position to confront the evil of secular influences, their lives spoke eloquently of the priority of faith over compromise to negative secular influences. Most Christians, however, addressed the sacred-secular tension by continuing to live their daily lives within a secular society. They were supported in doing this by participation in their faith community. With guidance of the Spirit, prayer, and sometimes heated discussion, community leaders formulated decisions that served to guide the community on a variety of issues facing the early Christians. Just as community membership and participation, dialogue, leadership, and guidance served the first Christians, so these may well serve today's Christians facing questions from the secular environment in which they live and work. Active participation in a faith community can support disciples today who value their spiritual growth.

Concerns of the Early Church

Another concern of the early leaders of the Christian community was whether to retain members who were unfaithful during times of persecution or who were lax in practicing their faith. Because of overwhelming pressure from persecution and the pagan social environment, Christians strayed in their moral practice. Three sins in particular — idolatry, adultery, and homicide — raised controversy among the leaders of the community. The seriousness of the offense warranted severe measures but ones that reflected Jesus' message of repentance and forgiveness. Accordingly, church communities or authorities could expel or excommunicate a member for grave sins both to challenge the person and also to prevent scandal in the community. However, if the sinner actually repented there was no Christian consensus on how, or even if, the person could be accepted back into the community. Some type of penitential discipline seemed in order, but the kind and length of the penance became a controversial topic. Church Fathers like Justin the Martyr (d. ca. 165), Tertullian (d. ca. 220), St. Ignatius of Antioch (d. ca. 220), St. Clement of Alexandria (d. 216), Origen (d. 253), and St. Cyprian (d. 258) addressed such moral issues as cooperation with pagan worship, production of pagan idols by Christian artisans, licentious theatrical productions, lewd fashions, military service in pagan armies, and cruelty in circuses.[1] Many of the questions on penitential discipline were resolved at the Council of Nicaea in A.D. 325. Under the leadership of the emperor Constantine, this council determined that excommunicated persons, those who left the church during persecutions, and others who had abandoned Christianity (apostates) could be readmitted to the community after appropriate periods of penance (see table 5, which summarizes the Patristic Era).

The early Christians faced periods of persecution that challenged their beliefs. Many were killed because of their faith and became martyrs because of the stands they took. Their martyrdom was a supreme witness of moral rectitude in the face of evil and possibly death. The persecutions strengthened rather than weakened the early church, for the inspirational "seeds of martyrs" brought new growth to the early Christian community.

Several written works of the Patristic Era contain moral concepts that have withstood the test of time. The writings of St. Ambrose and of St. Augustine are particularly important. St. Ambrose (d. 397) was the first to write a systematic work on moral theology. St. Augustine (d. 430) wrote extensively on the moral life. Basing many of his teachings on personal struggles to lead a moral life, Augustine wrote his *Confessions* and *The City of God,* which contain treatises on morality. In these he simply and candidly admits to lapses in the moral life. Augustine had led a sexually promiscuous lifestyle for a period of time and became involved in a Manichaean group that upheld heretical beliefs. In time Augustine came to believe that the moral life is to lead the believer toward love of God and finally to eternal union with God. Even after his conversion to Christianity, Augustine struggled with his heretical Manichaean past, and he was not able to completely free himself of the influences of this ascetic and anti-body heretical group.[2] Their negative views on the body

---

Table 5
The Patristic Era

Leaders

Apostles, scriptural writers
Hierarchy — popes, bishops
Fathers of the Church
Monastic leaders

Concerns of the Community

Idolatry, adultery, homicide
Apostasy
Philosophical, religious, cultural influences
Pagan practices

---

and physical creation tainted his writings on sexual ethics, an area that he battled with personally during the period of his conversion. Augustine's views on sexuality have had a major influence, for good and for ill, on Christianity even till today.[3]

Latent Period

Some refer to the next period, from about 700 to 1100, as the Dark Ages or Latent Period because there was little advancement in theology and church teaching. This period could be regarded as "a settling in" time. Heresies had been challenged, and many church teachings and much dogma had been clarified and defined through various councils. The monastic movement grew and exercised great influence in the church by defining what was the right and holy way to live, which in some sense defined the moral way to live.

There was, however, a major breakthrough in terms of penance and penitential practices with the emergence of the Celtic penitential movement during the Latent Period. This movement concentrated on penance for sin as a means to holiness. No longer dealing with holiness from a monastic perspective, priests were concerned about private confession and the types of penances that should be imposed for sin. The preoccupation with sin in Christianity can be traced to this movement. Conversion from sinful ways had always been important to morality, but the penitential movement gave it central focus. The movement evolved from one of the practices of monasticism, the private confession and forgiveness of sins. The superior or an older monk could, in private confession, issue penances to the penitent monk as a part of the confession of sins.

In time the practice of auricular or private confession spread to the laity, who went to their local parish priest for confession and remission of sins. By the sixth century, penitential books provided priests with a tariff of penances prescribed for various sins. The books included lists of questions to guide confessors, classification of sins, and advice about dealing with penitents. Irish missionaries carried the books to the Frankish countries, England, Italy, and Spain, where they became known as Irish penitentials. In these ways, private, auricular confession and doing penance for sin became widely practiced in the church.

The penitentials are criticized today for their stress on sin rather than virtue, for their rigid approach to sin, and for their imposition of harsh penances that did not reflect the mercy and compassion of a forgiving God. "The usual forms of self-mortification enjoined were fasts of varying intensity and duration, deprivation of sleep, multiple genuflections and recitations of psalms, long periods of standing or of silence, different degrees of discomfort at night, beatings, and, of course, sexual abstinence."[4] Sometimes wealthy sinners were required to give their excess to the poor, give alms, and release their slaves. Others who might be too ill to perform the imposed penances could "redeem" the penance through philanthropy, "buying back prisoners of war, releasing slaves, and in later centuries, building churches and monasteries or endowing colleges."[5] A later development was penance by proxy, in which someone, even a priest and monk, was paid to perform penances, a practice that led to trafficking in indulgences and making pilgrimages. The entire system lent itself to abuses that Martin Luther protested and that contributed to the Reformation.

High Middle Ages

The next period of Christian history, from 1100 to 1300, was one of "conspicuous" growth in theology compared to the previous period of latency. Growth in theology was encouraged by the Fourth Lateran Council. It was convoked by Innocent III in 1215 and was a landmark meeting of the world's twelve hundred bishops. The council dealt with many important issues, but one in particular pertained to conversion in the moral life. It highlighted participation in the sacraments of Penance and Eucharist and their importance in moral conversion through performance of the "Easter duties."[6]

At the council, the secrecy of the confessional was enjoined on all confessors with strict penances imposed on anyone who "broke the seal of the confessional." Some contend that by requiring yearly confession of parishioners, the council really tried to help parish priests determine who was truly a Catholic, an *active* member of the church.

A further result of the Fourth Lateran Council was to classify and summarize all literature on theological practices and topics into handbooks. Consequently, summas for confessors, compendiums, and confessional literature came into existence. These writings were more scholarly and theological than the penitential books. The summas did not give separate treatment to moral theology but rather treated moral topics under theological themes such as God, creation, the fall, incarnation, and the sacraments. One example of such writings was the *Decrees* of Gratian, which summarized all the canons or laws being used by the church.

Outstanding theologians of the time included St. Bonaventure (d. 1274) and St. Thomas Aquinas (d. 1274), both of whom wrote brilliantly and extensively on theological questions. Aquinas masterfully synthesized his theology in his *Summa Theologiae*. Although his theology, presented in question-and-answer form, was originally rejected, Aquinas's work was subsequently vindicated and came to be the primary source for theological study in seminaries until Vatican II. Aquinas based his work on scripture and the writings of the early Church Fathers such as Augustine and Tertullian. He also integrated Christian beliefs with the best in pagan philosophical writings, especially the philosophy of Aristotle. The theology of Aquinas is grounded in two complementary sources — nature, or the realm of human reason, and the supernatural realm of faith and God's grace. For Aquinas there is an eternal law of God, or internal order of creation, that directs all creatures to their ultimate goal, which is union with God. Aquinas believed that "in every soul, as in every body, there is a weight drawing it constantly, moving it always to find its natural place of rest; and this weight we call love."[7] Through God's grace and human cooperation the universe is redeemed and brought to union with God.

Aquinas wrote a systematic explanation of natural law that is still a fundamental concept of Roman Catholic moral theology. Natural law is a philosophical concept different from "law" understood as a legal norm decided by a judiciary body. Rather, natural law is based on the nature of human beings. When we observe the physical nature of a human being, it is obvious that humans use reason to direct their actions and make decisions. This aspect of natural law is sometimes called "the order of reason" because what is morally right is determined by what is reasonable for a human person and for society. It is also obvious to an observer that generally all human beings share physical functions such as procreation, protection of the young, and self-preservation. Physical functions common to human beings are another aspect of natural law called "the order of nature." This reading of natural law determines what is morally right in issues pertaining to our bodies such as health, sexuality, procreation, and marriage. The church uses both approaches to natural law in its teachings.

Aquinas believed natural law is inherent in human beings and is placed there by God, who is reflected in each creature. Understanding that all things come from God and lead us to God, Aquinas believed a human person could know God and what God expects ("God's will") by the use of reason. Because of the ability to reason, human beings are capable of knowing and accepting the divine order and destiny within themselves and creation.

Natural law is often expressed as "do good and avoid evil." We are to seek the good in all things and in all persons and then do good as dictated by our conscience. The good is defined as those authentic inclinations and satisfactions toward which human beings are essentially and naturally oriented by their nature as human beings.[8]

In terms of theology, this means that people using their practical reason, aided by grace, can know and participate in the eternal plan for creation and apply this to the everyday situations of life. Reason includes observation and research, intuition, emotions, and an aesthetic sense that direct us to know human reality in all of its goodness and truth. Reason helps us grasp what it means to be fully human and to evaluate human experiences. This inclusive, holistic understanding of reason has been used in many of the papal teachings pertaining to society. Encyclicals like *Sollicitudo Rei Socialis* and *Centesimus Annus* are based on the "order of reason" and include teaching about care for the poor, participation in government, and just wages.

Natural law interpreted from the "order of nature" is concerned with matters related to physical nature. Again, reason is used, but the process follows nature's laws observed in the physical makeup and rhythms of life. For this reason, the dictum "Fish swim, birds fly" has been used by some to describe this reading of natural law.

We are to follow the physical nature of a creature to know what is morally right without requiring or imposing what is not natural on creatures. Aquinas followed our biological nature to determine what is natural for a human being: eyes are to be used for seeing, hands for manipulating objects. This understanding was based on knowledge of the human body and its natural processes, knowledge from which developed the church's norms on medical ethics and sexual ethics. God created the human being in a certain way; any intervention to change this is to act against God's law. To obey natural law, as interpreted by the church, is to obey God; to disobey natural law is to disobey God.

Later generations of scholars, called Thomists, used the writings of Aquinas on natural law to form intricate systems of judgment about moral cases. This case study method of moral discussion is called casuistry. Far removed from the original manuscripts of the *Summa* and the intentions of Aquinas, these scholars at times undervalued or ignored the original depth and breadth of Aquinas. During the Renaissance and modern period, those theologians whose work was derived from the writings of Aquinas were called the Scholastics or "Schoolmen." Their theological method, known as Scholasticism, was used by scholars in their commentaries on Aquinas and in theological treatises.

While all this was going on at the university level, the average parish priests were busy ministering to parishioners' needs, hearing confessions, and administering absolution. Confession of sin, penances, pilgrimages, and indulgences all assisted the Christian pilgrim in attaining heaven. The moral life largely focused on sin and the removal of sin rather than on conversion. At the same time the study of scripture receded as the penitential practices grew. While commentaries on the *Summa* increased, the scriptural foundations for theology decreased. It took centuries before scripture again gained a balance with tradition in the development of theology and the moral life.

Contemporary Eye on the Past:
Materialism

New cars, TVs, computers, stereo equipment, boats, clothes, gourmet food, and jewelry flood the advertisement sections of the newspapers. TV programs are interrupted every few minutes with several commercials that appeal to the appetites of viewers. Most of what is advertised is not essential for human life. Americans generally have their basic needs met, so the commercials are geared to the "extras" that would make life fun, comfortable, luxurious, and exciting. Even if we have an item, we are encouraged by the media to get another, for "more is better" seems to be the guiding rule for advertising. More sales encourage the growth of the economy, but more material things lead to materialism, a mentality that makes material goods the goal of life. Materialism is more than simply the accumulation of things — they become the stairway to power. Even while we know money — and things — cannot buy happiness, we continue to be duped by the materialism rampant in our society. Although we do not need many of the things we buy, we still buy them; then we buy better quality items from big name stores; and finally we buy items for the sake of prestige. We want name brands that set us apart and above others.

The competition for sales is part and parcel of our capitalist society. Numerous encyclicals and pastoral letters have been written decrying the spiritual problem of materialism so prevalent in our era. Still it continues. Were there societies in the past that confronted materialism? This was a spiritual problem during the period of history we just studied. Like today, in the High Middle Ages the gap between the "haves and have-nots" had widened. There were a few very wealthy citizens and legions of very poor peasants. The wealthy landowners lived in castles, owned large plots of land, and hired peasants to run their property. The peasants were usually uneducated and illiterate, lived in hovels, and were mistreated in terms of living conditions and pay. Superstition held a strong sway in the absence of education, and religion was often a mixture of magic and faith. Belief in the saints centered around their ability to perform miracles after certain regimens of prayer and fasting were performed. The churches were in disrepair, and genuine faith in God was in decline.

In the midst of this social scenario entered Francis of Assisi, the Poverello. Born of a rich merchant, Francis denounced the riches of his father and claimed God as his only Father. From the point of this public declaration, Francis began to beg so he could feed the poor and led a life of utter poverty. His lifestyle of prayer and austerity was appealing to those who wanted personal meaning and a deeper happiness than material things could provide. Within a short time,

Francis had many followers, including a woman, Clare, who influenced women attracted to a life of poverty. "Holy Lady Poverty" was embraced by the followers of Francis and served as a witness to gospel values of loving God first and foremost, care for the poor and needy, and simplicity of life. The radical conversion of Francis affected the citizens of Assisi and, indeed, anyone who heard of him and his followers. Eventually Francis established the Franciscan order to witness in a radical way to the kind of joyous life that can be found in following Jesus, a life of happiness not based on material things. Poverty and simplicity of life confronted materialism.

Others embraced similar lifestyles to the Franciscans and, like them, confronted the spiritual problems of society. Followers of Dominic preached the Word of God and defended the church, which was under attack by heretics. St. Thomas Aquinas was a Dominican whose scholarly work, as we noted above, serves the church to this day. Still others continued the work of rebuilding places of worship and correcting abuses in religious devotions through the study of theology.

Commitment in discipleship to Jesus, preaching of the Word of God, and worship were the correctives for this earlier era of materialism. Today we see efforts at renewal continuing after Vatican II, particularly through the efforts of the pontiff John Paul II. He urges Christians to think globally rather than individualistically and to realize that all people are our brothers and sisters no matter where they live. The pope believes solidarity with the poor will lead to international sharing of resources and technology so that all will live in human dignity. He says, "The goods of this world are originally meant for all." The "preferential option for the poor," he believes, will lead the wealthy to consider the common good rather than continue to accumulate wealth and power. Through solidarity with the poor, whether they are poor individuals or poor countries, we will find the peace and happiness we have mistakenly sought in material things (*Sollicitudo Rei Socialis* 40–43).

Renaissance Period

The Renaissance, which ran roughly from the fourteenth to the seventeenth centuries, was a time of rejuvenation for the arts and literature. Modern science can trace its beginnings to the Renaissance. Moral theology was also influenced by the resurgence of study and intellectual investigation during this period. New emphasis was placed on the meaning and dignity of the individual and the development of persons, important topics for moral thinking about our human and humane life.

Nominalism. Two significant changes in society affected theology: a philosophical move from Scholasticism to nominalism and a shift in economy from medieval feudalism to middle-class commerce. The philosophical move to nominalism included the belief that human beings were incapable of grasping universal concepts. Therefore they could not grasp objective reality such as laws and moral norms. Since this belief held that only the individual person could determine reality, the consequence was relativism. All morality was determined by the individual; moral norms could not determine the common good. Because humans could not understand law, power was the only alternative to establish order. Tyranny that imposed conformity by power was a natural consequence of the nominalist philosophy.

This philosophy affected moral theology by promoting the notion that one could not discuss the Christian moral life or predict intrinsically good or bad acts. Nominalists believed individual persons determined what was morally right or wrong. With this strong emphasis on the individual subject, objective goals or laws were downplayed in determining the morality of an act. The nominalists contributed to ethical individualism by stressing the person and the individual moral act. The nominalists did a detailed analysis of individual acts to determine their justice or injustice. Casuistry was a natural outcome of this philosophy because it evaluated moral acts isolated from a broader spectrum of community and society. Solidarity with others, community, and social dimensions of behavior had little influence in deciding the morality of an act.

Reform of the Church. Martin Luther (d. 1546), a devout Roman Catholic priest of the Augustinian order, was keenly aware of the suffering of the peasant class under the medieval feudal system. The poor were living in abominable conditions, and more oppressive still were the religious restrictions they suffered. They were too poor to "buy" indulgences or to hire others to do the required penances to have their sins forgiven. As a consequence, they believed they were damned for all eternity. This dire religious situation, combined with the law-centered mentality of the age, inspired Luther to challenge the religious leaders of the Roman Church. In a time when salvation seemed to be based on strict rules determining who was justified, Luther taught no one was just; when people measured morality by the law, Luther used St. Paul's writings to dispute the law. He emphasized grace, faith, and reliance on God's mercy in the face of a church that he accused of requiring good works to "earn" heaven.

The implications for moral theology were vast. During this turbulent time, morality was based primarily on individualism, on law, and on strict justice; the social and communal dimensions of morality were downplayed or ignored. This perspective did not encourage conversion of heart that would move the believer beyond self-centered interests to a consideration of others. A loving heart would encompass the needs of the poor, the sick, and the needy. However, a minimalist mentality — rather than generous care and giving to others — was prevalent at the time.

In this climate of challenge from Luther, and with numerous problems facing the church, the Council of Trent was convened from 1545 to 1563. It was a Counter-Reformation council meant to contain the rebellion and to counter the challenges brought by the protesting groups. "Much of Europe had been lost to the church, and the first priority was to establish the line of demarcation with clarity."[9] One line of demarcation between the Roman Catholic Church and the Protestant churches affected moral theology. The Catholic seminary system was to clearly define and strengthen moral theology. A system of formal education for all clergy was established and required for all candidates preparing for priesthood. The focus of study was on the uniqueness of Catholicism as different from Protestantism. Moral theology became a systematized discipline of Roman Catholic studies "aimed only at a specific and detailed presentation of the requirements of the Christian life."[10] Like the nominalist philosophy of the time, even this official Roman Catholic moral theology concentrated on isolated acts and offered a minimalist view of salvation. It considered those acts that were necessary and required for salvation. Moral theology no longer had as its basis a reflection on scripture and the mysteries of the faith but contained more of the specifics and characteristics of canon law.[11]

Contemporary Eye on the Past:
Individualism

Centuries after the Renaissance, we live with many laws and norms that are not unlike some aspects of that era. We have a judiciary system to interpret the laws and theologians to interpret church teaching for us. Nevertheless, many in society dislike being told what to do no matter who is doing the interpretation. Some believe their education and experience enable them to make decisions as valid as those dictated by someone with authority. Individualism concentrates on the "me and my interests," largely excluding the views of others. With individualism, objective values encased in laws and moral terms are considered less important than individual interpretation and application of the laws. Personal views take priority over the objective views of others in society or in church leadership whose task it is to apply and interpret laws.

Examples of individualism can be found readily in society today. Many consider morals to be a private matter, not to be determined in the public arena. We find this view prevalent in arguments for abortion that say it is a woman's decision and a private matter. Not even the father of the fetus is given a legal voice in the woman's decision to have an abortion. Moral individualism is operative when couples choose to live together without seeking public and community endorsement provided through a marriage license and ceremony. We could also cite situations in business and medicine where decisions are made primarily or only for the profit of the owner or to increase the power of a group, rather than for the common good.

Society still endorses the popular dictum of individualism, "If it feels good, do it." The result is relativism, a necessary correlative of moral individualism that has left Generation X with few anchorholds to guide them morally. They long for traditions and norms to assist them in establishing a stable moral life.

How did the people of the Renaissance deal with individualism and its consequent partner, relativism? People of that era had to deal with the problems of nominalism through some overdrawn movements such as the voluntarist movement and legalism. These two movements effected the antilaw mentality of nominalism. On the one hand, in voluntarism, I rely on my will to do something: "I do it because *I* want to do it, not because the law requires me to do it." People can volunteer to do the right thing, but they cannot be forced by law to do the morally right thing. Legalists, on the other hand, looked to the law as the sole determiner of right, even though the law was minimalist in its demands. This mentality of voluntarism and legalism also infiltrated Christian morality and spirituality.

The Renaissance teaches that extreme positions like voluntarism and legalism can increase problems rather than solve them. It teaches that wisdom and truth are more often found in moderate approaches to individualism. While some groups today are pushing for extreme measures that are legalistic in tone, other groups are taking a lax, relativistic attitude toward guidance from authority. The church is guiding its disciples with a more balanced approach by urging them to consider the common good and to be community-minded. The social teaching of the church does this explicitly, as do the teachings on sexuality, which seek a communal perspective. Personal values and personal decisions are important and are strengthened when the entire body of believers and nonbelievers is considered.

The Modern Era: Moral Theology Comes of Age

A Discipline in Its Own Right. The Reformation and the Counter-Reformation ushered in and set the parameters for the modern era of moral theology. Between 1600 and 1960 there was great need for pastoral care: following the Reformation, the laity sought direction and clarity in the midst of spiritual and theological upheavals. To prepare clergy for this work, writers began to produce texts that incorporated the strengths of the speculative theological summas of the university thinkers and the summas used by confessors. One such author was John Azor, whose *Institutiones Morales* (1603) contains the fundamentals of moral theology, the theology of the sacraments, and ecclesiastical penalties. These writers no longer used dogmatic theology, which reflected on the mysteries of the faith, as a basis for moral theology. Instead there was a shift toward using canon law as a basis for moral theology.[12]

Manuals and Casuistry. Moral theology took the format of the manuals, which continued in use until Vatican II. The manuals contained succinct teachings on moral issues, guided confessors, and served as reference books to help people examine their consciences. "In spite of their several undoubted merits, they were largely responsible for the legalistic, minimalistic and casuistic trends in Catholic moral theology that dominated the scene until Vatican II."[13] The manuals used casuistry, a method of judging the morality of an action based on "cases." The cases were seen as "typical situations" that included defined circumstances and a solution based on the exact situation and the specified circumstances.

This method of problem solving proved to be both beneficial and detrimental. It benefited those who wanted a simple, straightforward answer and who did not have enough knowledge to arrive at a moral decision on their own. Casuistry was also helpful in guiding confessors and parishioners through moral quandaries because it offered clear solutions. It did, however, foster legalism and minimalism — "the letter of the law" was observed but not the spirit of the law.

During the early years of this period, the clergy received minimal education and formation. For their pastoral and confessional ministries, they needed the assistance of the concise and precise answers that the manuals provided. Casuistry enabled the clergy to make moral judgments based on the analysis of more educated theologians, which ensured they gave sound moral advice. However, casuistry was unable to deal with new complexities of moral problems, especially those introduced by advances in science, psychology, and sociology. These have introduced untold numbers of circumstances and conditions that must be considered individually before a moral judgment can be made. In these circumstances casuistry is of little help because it is inflexible. It can judge the morality of an act uncontaminated by new circumstances. In a system of casuistry there necessarily have to be principles that are unchanging and acts that can always be judged right or wrong. These are called moral absolutes, those actions clearly defined as morally right or wrong, allowed or not allowed.

Another inadequacy of casuistry is that it does not promote conversion but too often encourages a type of legalism. If actions rather than intentions are the focal point of judging morality, then the root of conversion found in one's thinking and attitude is untouched even though one performs "morally right actions." Casuistry is inadequate for moral conversion because it gives insufficient attention to the many factors of a moral decision. As stated earlier, the three font principle attends to all the factors of an act: the act itself, the intention of the actor, and the circumstances surrounding the act. In a casuistic approach, less attention is given to the intention and the circumstances of the act. The intention rests in a person's heart and mind, and it is these that must be converted if an act is to reflect the Christian morality of a person. While casuistry gives some weight to intention and circumstances, its exaggerated use leads to moral legalism and a rigid, unchanging application of morality, no matter what the contemporary situation might be. With the advent of Vatican II, this extreme was corrected.

One example of this legalistic situation was found in the Sunday Mass obligation that required parishioners to be present in the church for the "three main parts" of the Mass: Offertory, Consecration, and Communion. Some readers may recall parishioners who visited in the vestibule of the church until the priest's sermon was finished, after which they came into the body of the church to be present for the Offertory. Invariably they left immediately after Communion was distributed. These parishioners had fulfilled their obligation, but they lacked the spirit of the requirement and missed out on the communal dimension of liturgical prayer and a sense of the importance of the scriptural readings. A major fault of the manualist system sprang from the attitudes it frequently engendered: legalism, rationalism, and minimalism. If the exact specifications of the case were met, then a person had done the "right" thing even if the spirit of the requirement had not been fulfilled.

Three developments occurred because of casuistry. The first development emerged as a reaction to casuistry and its downplaying of the subjective element in moral decision making. With an excessive emphasis on the subject, the laxist development took a casual attitude toward objective moral norms and looked more to the individual person deciding right and wrong. Casuistry did not allow much room for subjective elements such as conscience, although in an attempt to bring subjective factors into play, its proponents did allow some exceptions, and some laws were considered doubtful. A second development, tutiorism or probabiliorism, produced an opposite reaction — a rigid conformism to moral norms. It was led by Jansenists, who did not believe in freedom of the will but rather believed in moral determinism and held puritanical views toward sex. They upheld probabiliorism, a rigorist opinion toward the law that expected exact obedience no matter what the circumstances of the action. In this view, subjective elements of moral decision making were eliminated or minimized. The extreme positions of laxism and rigorism were later condemned by the church. St. Alphonsus Liguori, the patron saint of moral theologians, proposed a middle route between law and rigorism and between freedom of conscience and laxism. His proposal of equiprobabilism balanced the two and quieted the theological storm of the period.

Summas, manuals, legalism, minimalism, and rationalism were used in the moral theology of the Counter-Reformation church. The many efforts to strengthen moral theology came from the concrete situations of pastors and social situations of the time, but each effort also had its negative outcome. As moral theology became more precise in delineating moral right and wrong through the use of casuistry, a minimalist mentality grew among the faithful. When parameters were clearly defined regarding moral right and wrong, one could take the parameters as the fulfillment of the law. This minimalist mentality was fed by rationalism. Some of these problems were addressed when a renewal of the church and its theology began with Vatican II. However, some of these problems have prevailed even until today because they are embedded in the human condition.

Renewal Begins

Long before Vatican II opened in 1963, there were signs of renewal in theology. Scriptural foundations for theology were requisite if theological work was to continue, so there was a need for theological renewal. The Tübingen School in Germany is credited with some of the earliest efforts of renewal under Johann Michael Sailer (1751–1832), the bishop of Regensburg. Sailer and Johann Baptist Hirscher (1788–1865), another leader in renewal, studied the work of early church leaders and scripture scholars and believed scripture could help renew moral theology. After the Reformation, scripture scholarship largely became the domain of Protestant scholars, not of Catholic theologians, the latter being bent on defending the theological and dogmatic tradition. The Tübingen theologians returned to the scriptures to highlight New Testament concepts such as conversion and discipleship.

At the same time there was a renewed interest in spirituality, which led theologians to retrieve the writings of the early church leaders. "Finally, and perhaps most importantly, they demanded a reunification of moral theology and dogmatic theology; they sought to reestablish the truly theological roots of Christian ethics."[14]

But these early efforts at renewal in moral theology were slow-paced. A major event in the history of the period was Vatican I (1870), which dealt with many church issues, one of which affects the teaching office of the church today, that is, the definition of infallibility. The council did not address moral theology, but renewal continued through the work of individual scholars such as Joseph Mausbach (1861–1931) and Theodore Steinbuchel (1888–1949). Two contemporary German contributors who taught at Roman universities were Bernard Häring, C.Ss.R. (b. 1912), at the Alphonsinum, and Josef Fuchs, S.J. (b. 1912), at the Gregorianum. Their careful and outstanding work in the Roman universities contributed greatly to the renewal of moral theology. Häring and Fuchs assisted the Council Fathers who took the next major step in theological renewal at Vatican II.

Conclusion

The history of Christian morality is bound up with society's mores, social conditions, and historic events. The church, its leaders, and·the disciples of Jesus stand as teachers and witnesses to truth and gospel values. At times the stand taken by Christians has been difficult and painful, in each century and era of history. In retrospect, we can also see the emergence of truth from the turmoil and the triumph of good over evil. At other times, it is easy to spot the weakness and frailty of human nature in leaders and movements of society. Mistakes and moral deterioration occurred that required honesty and then renewal on the part of church leaders and members.

Today we reap the rich harvest of wisdom gleaned from the suffering and deaths of our Christian ancestors who witnessed to moral truth. We see how they established foundations for our faith, and we have lessons to learn for our day. With a "contemporary eye on the past" we see lessons in different eras that apply today as we struggle with issues of materialism, individualism, and secularism. In learning these lessons we create a new world tuned ever more finely to the vision of Christ for all people.

Notes

1. George V. Lobo, S.J., *Guide to Christian Living* (Westminster, Md.: Christian Classics, 1984), 3.

2. Begun by Manes about A.D. 276, the Manichaean sect held a syncretistic view of religious dualism and gnosticism. Dualists maintain "the general theological view that all reality is composed of, and arises from, distinct, absolutely independent, antagonistic, and coequal principles: Good and Evil." Gnosticism, one of the earliest Christian heresies, "denied the reality of the incarnation. Besides stressing the role of saving knowledge, it also denied the goodness of creation and of the material order" (Richard P. McBrien, *Catholicism* [San Francisco: Harper, 1994], 1238, 1240). Manichaeans taught that the spirit could be released from matter through asceticism. This view was renounced by Christianity as a heresy.

3. See John Mahoney, *The Making of Moral Theology* (Oxford: Clarendon Press, 1987), 58–68, and Lisa Sowle Cahill, *Between the Sexes* (New York: Paulist Press, 1985), 112–14.

4. Mahoney, *Making of Moral Theology*, 10.

5. Ibid., 11.

6. "On reaching the age of discernment, everyone of the faithful, of either sex, is faithfully at least once a year to confess all his sins in private to his own priest, and is to take care to fulfill according to his abilities the penance enjoined on him, reverently receiving the sacrament of the Eucharist at least at

Easter. ... Otherwise he is to be barred from entering the church in his lifetime and to be deprived of Christian burial at his death" (DS 813).

7. Etienne Gilson, _The Christian Philosophy of St. Thomas Aquinas_ (New York: Random House, 1956), 134.

8. Mahoney, _Making of Moral Theology_, 80.

9. Timothy O'Connell, _Principles for a Catholic Morality_ (San Francisco: Harper and Row, 1990), 18.

10. Ibid., 18.

11. Ibid., 19.

12. Canon law is a body of regulations, standards, or norms accepted by the church for its governance. These canons include such regulations as those governing the administration of the sacraments, church property, and members of religious orders. The first compilation of canons was done by Gratian in the twelfth century; canon law was revised after Vatican II, in 1983, in order to make the canons consonant with the teachings of the council.

13. Lobo, _Guide_, 9.

14. O'Connell, _Principles_, 20.

Chapter 9

RENEWAL OF MORAL THEOLOGY

To understand the recent renewal of theology one must understand the climate of society and the church prior to Vatican II. The 1960s were filled with an atmosphere of turmoil and excitement. In the United States there was turmoil in the form of protests against the Vietnam War and marches and demonstrations aimed at achieving civil rights for all. There was excitement in the hopes and efforts to create new structures of justice, freedom, and peace for all citizens. Something new was being born, just as something old seemed to be passing away.

Educational and governmental structures that protected the rights of the system were challenged, and in some cases institutions closed before the impact of demonstrators who demanded individual rights. University administrators were unseated, and police officers were attacked. Educational institutions were closed and alternative colleges set up; the offices of college and university presidents were occupied by students who demanded comprehensive changes in the curriculum and policies of schools. Young men opposed to the draft challenged the military and government leadership of the United States. A national Democratic political convention was the scene of protests that the police could not contain. Most disturbing were assassinations at the highest level of government and leadership: President John F. Kennedy, Attorney General Robert Kennedy, and civil rights leader Martin Luther King Jr. Personalism took center stage in philosophy, literature, politics, and social movements. Morally, the motto became "What fulfills and makes a person happy is what is right." However, with emphasis on personal morality, this "right" was not balanced with objective morality represented by laws and authority. Law and authority were part of the "establishment" being rejected. Given the force of widespread protests, major institutions of leadership were compelled to evaluate their entire system and offer new or revised products and services. The climate for a "new order" was in the air.

In the midst of this turmoil and excitement in Western countries,

Pope John XXIII opened Vatican II in 1963. With this ecumenical council, the pope ushered in a massive renewal of the Roman Catholic Church. For the first time in the church's history, three thousand bishops from all over the world were able to attend sessions with *periti* (experts in theology) for a two-year period. There was excitement among the delegates just as there was in society. The pope and bishops, with the help of their theological advisors, opened the dusty windows of the church to the world and let in fresh air.

Theologians who had pursued contemporary questions pertaining to theology were called on to offer their expertise. Recognized as experts in their field were theologians Karl Rahner, S.J., Bernard Häring, C.Ss.R., Yves Congar, O.P., Henri de Lubac, Hans Urs von Balthasar, Marie Dominique Chenu, O.P., whose thoughts enriched the deliberations of council delegates. Several members of the hierarchy proved to be significant leaders among the bishops: Leon-Josef Cardinal Suenens, Franz Cardinal König, and Johannes Cardinal Willebrands. American scholar John Courtney Murray, S.J., made significant contributions in the area of religious freedom. Other scholars who had studied contemporary issues in scripture and philosophy were ready to integrate their work with areas of theology. Indeed scriptural scholars were used in every aspect of theology from liturgy to ecclesiology. The renewal of theology was a renewal that sent the church back to its sources in scripture and the earliest traditions where the great mysteries of the faith were formulated. Commissions wrote and rewrote the documents of renewal until they were accepted by the delegates of the council.

Theology was renewed and the defensive posture of the Counter-Reformation church yielded to greater ecumenical dialogue. The presence of Protestant and non-Christian observers at the council bore dramatic witness to a spirit of openness to dialogue and renewal. And change the church did — although it would take decades to implement the renewal and to understand the foundational thinking behind the changes. It was not simply "change for change's sake" but was a change of necessity if the church was to continue to be a vibrant and significant force in contemporary society, if it was to meet the religious and pastoral needs of Christians.

Need for Change

Just what were the problems facing the church that required a breath of fresh air? By examining the status of the church one can recog-

nize the need for renewal. The church had maintained the riches
of tradition through the centuries and weathered the torrents of the
Reformation. Vatican I had formally acknowledged the power of the
pope to define doctrines as infallible. The hierarchical structure was
strong; answers were clearly defined in manuals available to confessors; and a casuistic approach predominated in moral theology. A
system of exceptions to the norm was in place so that virtually all
areas of morality could be handled through the norm or its exceptions. There were advantages to this system of morality: it was clear,
concise, and objective. By remaining almost solely in the objective
mode, the priest could interpret what was morally right or wrong
for all people, irrespective of culture and times and circumstances.
Intrinsic evil and moral absolutes were defined because they dealt
with objective data. Laws, another part of the objective approach
to moral theology, were defined with arguments from philosophy
to buttress every position. These seemingly air-tight arguments gave
less place for any subjective arguments of morality such as personal
conscience could raise.

However, there were also problems with this system of moral
theology. Life is dynamic, and the institutional church is a dynamic institution. This pervasive dynamism was evident in the rapid
changes after World War II, especially in the fields of communications, technology, science, and the arts. The dynamic life of
Christians who sincerely wished to follow the spirit of Christ forced
church leaders to come to terms with the vast amount of knowledge
and technology that posed new questions in morality. Traditional
approaches to moral theology could not adequately address these
questions, even with exceptions to the rules.

When the person and the community are taken seriously, as they
are at this period of time, a more historical approach to moral decisions is needed. In a historical approach, not only must the act
be discussed but equally important is the context of the person's
life and history. The moral act can no longer be isolated from the
circumstances and intentions of the persons involved in the moral decision. The subjective aspect of morality found in conscience has to
be balanced with the objective aspect of law. As an objective norm,
stipulations have to be balanced with the spirit of the law. Legalism
has to yield to conversion of heart and mind. Obedience cannot be
defined simply as compliance to the letter of the law but must include appropriation of the spirit of the law. When this is done, law
can truly contribute to the conversion of mind and heart.

Moral Theology according to Vatican II

Vatican II did not issue a document on moral theology. However, themes within all the documents displayed a new approach to moral theology. The Council Fathers placed moral theology within the context of dogmatic theology and scripture, rather than canon law. Traditional perspectives on natural law theory yielded to more contemporary interpretations that would more ably serve the moral life of the church. Importance was given to the individual person, to responsibility and freedom. Individual conscience, where moral freedom resides, was given due importance. To address the individual person, theologians had to address the context of the person's life and its historical dimensions. No longer could one make a moral judgment based solely on an act, but one had also to consider intention and circumstances. The renewal retrieved Aquinas's three font principle of act, intention, and circumstances, which brought a balance to the manualist mentality of previous eras that had focused primarily on the act isolated from the rest of a person's life and history.

Vatican II shifted the direction for doing theology from a "top-down" or deductive approach to include a more inductive approach. Church members were treated as adults who are themselves primarily responsible for their moral life rather than making the parish priest responsible for parishioners' moral decisions. Dialogue and learning with church authority were encouraged so adults could form their consciences and make mature moral decisions.

The Personalist and Communitarian Approach to Moral Theology

In addition to the shift in the approach to theology, there was also a shift in philosophy and literature known as the "turn to the subject," a movement of thought that recognized the importance of the person. Perhaps in response to the Industrial Revolution, which focused on "things" in the form of machines and mechanization rather than the "person," new emphasis was placed on the person in the post–Industrial Revolution. During the Industrial Revolution and in its wake, the rapid production of "things" for efficient and convenient use took on prime importance while the person working long hours in industry was minimized. The person was valued only insofar as he or she could produce at a rapid rate. Liberal capitalism had depersonalized workers in favor of increased production. The person in a factory was divorced from the product and so experienced no personal fulfillment in the production of goods. The worker performed monotonous and even demeaning types of repetitive work on the assembly lines of large factories.

The shift to "person" over "thing" could be found in the family as well as the arena of work. Playwright Henrik Ibsen uses the characters of Nora and Helmer to portray this "turn to the subject":

HELMER: This is monstrous! Can you forsake your holiest of duties in this way?

NORA: What do you consider my holiest of duties?

HELMER: Do I need to tell you that? Your duties to your husband and your children.

NORA: I have other duties equally sacred.

HELMER: Impossible! What duties do you mean?

NORA: My duties toward myself.

HELMER: Before all else you are a wife and mother.

NORA: That I no longer believe. I believe that before all else I am a human being, just as much as you are — or at least that I should try to become one.[1]

Nora defends her worth as a person. In moral theology, emphasis on the person gives a different hue to moral decisions. Criteria for what is morally right or wrong must square with an anthropology of the person and with psychological and sociological data about humanity. Such criteria have to consider variables that were excluded in the totally objective criteria of casuistry. All aspects of the person impinge on a moral action. Along with the moral act, one's culture, age, education, life experiences, and psychological state become relevant factors when one tries to make a moral decision. Bernard Häring took all of these factors into consideration when he stated, "One should never try to impose what the other person cannot sincerely internalize, except the case of preventing grave injustice toward a third person."[2] This contemporary moral theologian gives serious consideration to the situation of a person.

During the time of post–Vatican II renewal, many moral theologians retrieved the tradition of Thomas Aquinas, which emphasized the person. The moral theologian Louis Janssens developed personalist criteria that reflect the turn to the subject. Janssens states: "An action is morally right if it is beneficial to the person adequately considered in himself or herself (i.e., as an unique, embodied spirit) and in his or her relations (i.e., to others, to social structures, to the material world, and to God)."[3] The person and the context of a person's life must be considered in making moral decisions.

The Social Nature of the Person

One cannot address the person without taking into account the community in which the person resides. Living with other human beings in an ever-shrinking world makes communal perspectives unavoidable. The actions and attitudes of one person affect the lives of other people in ever-widening circles. Indeed, no person is an island. John Macmurray writes, "We live and move and have our being not in ourselves but in one another; and whatever rights or powers or freedom we possess are ours by the grace and favor of our fellows."[4] It is in community that people are most able to help each other be themselves.

The bishops of Vatican II emphasized the social and communal nature of the human person when, as noted earlier, they stated, "For by his innermost nature man is a social being, and unless he relates himself to others he can neither live nor develop his potential" (*Gaudium et Spes* 12). Moreover, as social beings, people learn to participate in the divine life, for they experience God in and through community. It is only through participation with each other that humans participate in the divine life. While it is important to consider the good of the person, that good must also benefit the whole. A common good must be sought such that the individual and the community both benefit. The principle of the common good found its roots in Thomas Aquinas and in the social teachings of the church beginning with Pius XI, but it took later popes to emphasize the common good over individual benefit and to show how that is applied in society today. Aquinas wrote:

> He who pursues the common good thereby pursues his own good, and for two reasons. First, because the proper good of the individual cannot exist without the common good of the family or state or realm.... Second, that since a person is a part of a household or state he ought to esteem that good for him which provides for the benefit of the community.[5]

Once a place is given to the person and to community, moral theology begins to take its ethical stands from a new perspective. Irish moralist Enda McDonagh has highlighted the new perspective and the moral responsibility Christians bear to create unity and community. McDonagh says the Word or self-giving of God to human beings forms humanity into a community. The true response each of us can make to God's gift is the promotion of community for all persons and their development as God's people.[6]

"Community" includes a person's local parish or faith community, the official church, and all the groups in society that have a moral impact on that person, that is, family, neighbors, friends, business associates, and others. These groups are external to the person but significant for the peace and well-being of the individual. Whatever the "community," it provides a place for the person to be and to establish identity and relationships. In terms of moral theology, the community furnishes the objective dimension of moral decision making, an important balance to the subjective dimension the person brings to moral decisions. Community membership widens the individual's perspective. It also foregrounds expectations of care and interest in the other members. The good of all must be considered. The common good becomes a concrete experience when one is committed to membership in any community group. Toward this end, some communities establish criteria, standards, norms, and even laws to regulate membership, funds, and activities. Besides the establishment of expectations, communities can be supportive, encouraging, inspiring, and helpful. The moral life based on faith can only exist within a faith community.

The turn to the subject in philosophy and literature certainly affected moral theology. Moral theology turned from an authority-grounded, law-oriented mode of morality to a mode that placed responsibility on the individual. In addition, the turn toward a dynamic, rather than a static, view of history enabled the council to include various disciplines of study such as science, history, psychology, and others in formulating moral statements. Because of vast developments in knowledge, change was acknowledged and expected, and church leaders largely avoided making definitive, static, absolutist statements. Theological disciplines moved toward dialogue with each other, reversing a trend toward isolation and compartmentalization. Interdisciplinary study was also pursued. Courses in psychology and religion, sociology and religion, environmental ethics, literature and religion, and world religions could be found on Catholic university curricula. Moral theology was particularly influenced by dialogue and study with biblical scholars. Biblical ethics emerged as a new discipline of study.

Biblical Roots of Moral Theology

Vatican II encouraged moralists to expand their study of moral theology. They were mandated to include scripture as well as natural law as foundations for moral theology. Since the council, scriptural ethics and revisionist readings of moral theology have emerged in response to the mandates of the council bishops. Because it contains the revealed Word of God, scripture is the foundation stone upon which all moral teachings are built. Scholarly tools are being employed to understand scripture and the moral teachings of Jesus. While recent scholarship can easily critique how scripture was used in the past, scripture is nonetheless central to any study of moral theology today.

Most warrants for moral behavior can be traced to a religious origin. This is especially true of the Jewish and Christian religions, which have extensive systems of moral theology. As a Jew, Jesus practiced the moral code of the Jewish religion and renewed it in his teaching and life practice. Christianity finds its roots in the Jewish religion and has incorporated much of its spirit. This is evident in the writings of the evangelists and Paul, a rabbinical disciple (Acts 22:3) and "Pharisee" (Phil. 3:5) who became an apostle of Jesus. Paul spoke from his traditional Jewish background, but faith in Jesus gave him a new interpretation and understanding of God's revelation. Paul saw Jesus as the fulfillment of the law. Jesus was the long-awaited Messiah who brought the Jewish people and others the good news, a new *evangelion:* all are saved and redeemed, not only members of the Jewish religion, who were the chosen race. More than the good news, Jesus introduced a new way of life. This meant Christianity was a new way of life that included a belief system, an outlook on creation and personal and relational life, and a moral perspective.

New Movements in Moral Theology

The faith community, like its individual members, experiences times of conversion. At certain periods in history, the community hears anew the call to discipleship and to commit its ways to Jesus Christ in more life-giving ways. A dramatic call to conversion was especially true of Vatican II. It was perhaps the first truly ecumenical council because it included bishops from the entire world, whereas Vatican I and the Council of Trent had limited attendance. The power of the ecumenical gathering is still evident today as Catholics continue to experience the spiritual and intellectual challenge of the documents and teachings of the Council Fathers in all areas of Christian life from liturgy to cultural development and family life. One could readily say that Vatican II was essentially a council of conversion.

One of the areas of conversion occurred in the church's stance toward members of other faiths and denominations. A posture of openness and acceptance by the Council Fathers, which is reflected in the document on ecumenism, was surely the work of the Spirit leading the church to conversion. The document acknowledges the presence of truth in all religions and the common search for truth shared by people of all faiths. In a spirit of respect and open dialogue, the documents challenge members of the church to a conversion of heart and mind: superiority of one religion is to yield to humility in the search for truth; a belief that salvation is only for members of the Catholic Church yields to the perception of all religious believers as loved by God; trust and dialogue are to be the modes of communication between believers; religious freedom means we are to respect the beliefs and religious practices of various religions. In this document alone, the moral conversion of a faith community undid the powers of sinful prejudice, pride, and self-righteousness. The "turn" of conversion was to the relational ways of Jesus: dialogue, respect, kindness, honesty. With the publication of Pope John Paul II's encyclical *Ut Unum Sint,* the spirit of conversion continued.

Still another example of conversion of the faith community was evident in the document *Gaudium et Spes.* So many aspects of the document show a new way of thinking that one can only marvel at the transformation of thought that occurred among the Council Fathers from the early drafts of the document until its final signing at the close of the council. One area of the document deserves special attention because of its impact on family life and marital spirituality. Faced with the growing pressures on family life and the instability of marriage, the Council Fathers changed the focus of marriage from legal foundations to biblical foundations. Marriage is to be a covenant, not a contract, and is to be based on a community of love of which God is the author. Procreation is as important as the relationship of love between the spouses. This shift of emphasis regarding the ends of marriage provides a solid basis for faithful marriages and

responsible parenthood. Children are gifts of God but the size of a
family is to be determined in responsible parenthood (*Humanae Vitae* 10). Sexual morality took a new direction from these "turns" in
moral theology given by the Council Fathers.

Vatican II and Renewal of Moral Theology

The basic conversion of thought at Vatican II involved the theocentric and Christocentric thrust of all the discussions, deliberations,
and documents. Christ was to be the center of all worship and theological study. The Christocentric emphasis naturally led to a focus on
the life of Jesus found in biblical theology. Moral theology, too, was
to be renewed in the light of scriptural study:

> Special attention needs to be given to the development of moral
> theology. Its scientific exposition should be more thoroughly
> nourished by scriptural teaching. It should show the nobility
> of the Christian vocation of the faithful, and their obligation to
> bring forth fruit in charity for the life of the world. (*Optatam
> Totius* 16)

This challenge required moral theologians to broaden the foundations and development of their study from a philosophical approach
to a scriptural approach. For the moral theologian this meant there
needed to be several shifts: a shift in the analysis of sin from a legalistic and manualist mentality to a scriptural one, from a focus on the
human act to a focus on the human person, from an orientation toward the sacrament of Penance to union with God in the Eucharist.
By calling for the nourishment of moral theology through scripture,
the council tried to "show the nobility of the Christian vocation
of the faithful, and their obligation to bring forth fruit in charity."
This implied a radical revision of moral theology, says Raymond F.
Collins, based on the scriptural roots of the Christian tradition. It
meant a retrieval of the medieval treatises on moral theology where
charity was the summit of the Christian life and the focus of vocations, particularly the lay vocation.[7] The emphasis on scriptural
foundations for moral theology opened lines of dialogue with non-
Catholic schools of theology that had taken a "gospel-social-virtue
approach" for many years. Ecumenical dialogue on moral issues
could be done more easily because of the common ground of scripture. *Unitatis Redintegratio* indicates the perspective of the Council
Fathers:

And if in moral matters there are many Christians who do not always understand the gospel in the same way as Catholics, and do not admit the same solutions for the more difficult problems of modern society, nevertheless they share our desire to cling to Christ's word as the source of Christian virtue and to obey the apostolic command: "Whatever you do in word or in work, do all in the name of the Lord Jesus Christ, giving thanks to God the Father through him" (Col 3:17). Hence, the ecumenical dialogue could start with discussions concerning the application of the gospel to moral questions. (23)

The council's dramatic challenge to renew moral theology along scriptural lines opened the door for a reexamination of the tradition of natural law as the foundation for moral theology.

Re-visioning the Natural Law Tradition

Natural law is a philosophical approach to reasoning that was used by the ancient philosophers. With carefully honed arguments, its deductions make logical sense. St. Augustine and later St. Thomas Aquinas used natural law theory. Thomas relied on Aristotle's approach to natural law and included it in his own system of theology in *Summa Theologiae*. With time the church saw natural law as "an expression of the will of God." Through the use of reason human beings search for truth and know the will of God in the truth of natural law. Thomas Aquinas said: "Natural law is simply the light of intelligence placed within us by God; by it we know what we should do and what we should avoid. God bestowed this light, or this law, with the creation" (*Dec. praec.* 1).

Vatican II's mandate to renew moral theology required a re-visioning of natural law. More than a philosophical system, Vatican II's understanding of natural law began to incorporate the mysteries of revelation and focused on Christ as the fullness of the Law. The *Catechism of the Catholic Church* (1992) continued to cast natural law in the context of scripture and Christ's teachings. The catechism states, "Moral law finds its fullness and unity in Christ. Jesus Christ himself is the way of perfection. He is the expression of the Law because he alone teaches and bestows God's justice: 'But the Law has found its fulfillment in Christ so that all who have faith will be justified' (Rm 10:4)." Moral theologians examined the fundamental concepts of natural law: definitions of the human, nature, natural order, reality, reason, and the physicalist approach of natural law. The Council Fathers encouraged use of the sciences and other branches of study and asked theologians "to look for a more appropriate way of communicating doctrine to the people of their time; since there is a difference between the deposit or the truths of faith and the manner in which they are expressed, keeping the same meaning and the same judgment" (*Optatam Totius* 16). Studies in renewal have shown the strengths of the natural law tradition but have also led to several critiques of natural law theory and affirmed the direction of the Council Fathers to give a broader foundation for moral thinking that includes scripture, supplemented by other disciplines of study.

For its basic moral teachings, the magisterium frequently uses the approaches to natural law proposed by the ancient philosophers Ulpian and Cicero.[8] However, recent popes have reflected a more "dynamic view" of natural law. This is evident in Paul VI's writings on the human person and community: "In the design of God, every man is called upon to develop and fulfill himself, for every life is a vocation.... By the unaided effort of his own intelligence and his will, each man can grow in humanity, can enhance his personal worth, can become more a person" (*Populorum Progressio* [1967]).[9] Still later, in 1971, Paul VI made one of the most important statements on subsidiarity, a statement that mirrored his use of natural law following "the order of reason" and his moral positions that are open to development:

> In the face of such widely varying situations it is difficult for us to utter a unified message and to put forward a solution which has universal validity. Such is not our ambition, nor is it our mission. It is up to the Christian communities to analyze with objectivity the situation which is proper to their own country, to shed on it the light of the Gospel's unalterable words, and to draw principles of reflection, norms of judgment and directives for action from the social teaching of the Church.[10]

Many contemporary moral theologians would prefer some integration of the two approaches to natural law: "the order of nature" approach used primarily in sexual and medical ethics and "the order of reason" approach found mainly in the social teachings of the church.[11] Many theologies have developed during the renewal time as attempts were made to displace the neo-Thomist approach to moral theology. New theological genres emerged from those theologians who tried "to revise and bring up to date the moral theology which dominated the discipline in the years of their seminary and graduate education."[12] The revisionists have taken different paths, which include an effort to understand Aquinas more adequately, use of the philosophies of Max Scheler and H. Richard Niebuhr, use of the insights of the Tübingen theologians, and finally a use of transcendental Thomism. Revisionist theologians have generally moved away from neo-Thomist models for doing theology.

Diversity and Tension in Moral Theology

The efforts at renewal have exposed a diversity of views on how moral theology should be studied as well as tensions in the tradition itself. While both of these may be constructive and lead to healthy dialogue, there is the danger of confusion for the laity who do not understand the theological and methodological distinctions of theologians and philosophers. The diversity can become hardened and polar positions can become entrenched such that theologians are no longer open to learn from each other. In addition, Pope John Paul II has feared some theologians are becoming relativists and rejecting the church's moral positions. His fears were expressed in the encyclical *Veritatis Splendor,* which addressed the widespread "overall and systematic calling into question of traditional moral doctrine on the basis of certain anthropological and ethical presuppositions" (4). The pope finds moral theologians abandoning "the traditional doctrine regarding the natural law and the permanent validity of its precepts," shunning certain of the church's moral teachings, and limiting the role of the magisterium in teaching morals. He fears people will make moral decisions out of a false sense of moral freedom. The reason for the encyclical is "to set forth, with regard to the problems being discussed, the principles of a moral teaching based upon Sacred Scripture and the living apostolic tradition, and at the same time to shed light on the presuppositions and consequences of the dissent which that teaching has met" (5).

The Pope finds that certain tendencies in contemporary moral theology, under the influence of the currents of subjectivism and individualism, involve novel interpretations of the relationship of freedom to the moral law, human nature, and conscience and that those tendencies also propose novel criteria for the moral evaluation of acts. Despite their variety, these tendencies are at one in lessening or even denying the dependence of freedom on truth (see no. 34). He states: "Although each individual has a right to be respected in his own journey in the search of the truth, there exists a prior moral obligation and a grave one at that to seek the truth and to adhere to it once it is known. As Cardinal John Henry Newman, that outstanding defender of the rights of conscience, forcefully put it: 'Conscience has rights because it has duties' " (34).

The pope is concerned about the use of freedom in moral decision making and tendencies toward subjectivism and individualism in contemporary moral theology. The voices of tension and dissent disturb the pope, who advises theologians to return to "sound doctrines" of the church.

One of the "sound doctrines" deserving more respect, says the pope, is the teaching authority of the church. Tension has erupted over the role of the bishops in their individual countries and the role of the bishop of Rome in relation to the body of bishops. At times the decisions of individual bishops have been called into question, and individual bishops have been put under scrutiny. Vatican II set out a model of authority for the church, calling it to practice subsidiarity and collegiality. As noted above, Paul VI followed the mind of the Council Fathers on subsidiarity when he said, "It is up to the Christian communities to analyze with objectivity the situation which is proper to their own country, to shed on it the light of the Gospel's unalterable words, and to draw principles of reflection, norms of judgment and directives for action from the social teaching of the Church."

A more prevalent problem in the church is the disregard of papal and magisterial authority on moral matters. Although numerous encyclicals and documents are issued to give guidance in moral matters, few are read or taken seriously. Frequently, the ordinary parishioner is not aware of the publication of magisterial documents, and seldom are these documents made available for parishioners to read. Besides the lack of knowledge about the magisterial teachings, disturbing attitudes exist. Some claim people do not attend to the church's teaching because there is a credibility gap between the hierarchy and the laity; others blame anticlericalism and antiauthority prejudices; still others point to the length and wordiness of the documents themselves; while others believe the magisterium has no right to speak on some moral matters, that is, sexual matters. There is a need to examine the attitudes toward church authority, freedom, individualism, and subjectivity, as the pope stated in *Veritatis Splendor*. A conversion of mind and heart is needed in the relationship between church members and their leaders.

Another area of tension in moral theology flows from the role of authority. The magisterium has the duty to specify the nature of moral wrong. Certain moral wrongs have been named as absolute moral prohibitions. That means these actions are serious moral wrongs under all circumstances. No explanations for these actions can constitute a morally right excuse for them. Examples of absolute moral wrongs include masturbation, artificial means of birth control, and homosexual acts. The issue seems to be that circumstances do not alter the nature of moral wrong in cases cited by the magisterium. Those who voice disagreement believe that circumstances will always alter the morality of an act and cannot be disregarded. What is also at issue is the fact that an act is declared morally wrong without any consideration of subjective involvement, the role of conscience, and personal choice. Again, conversion of mind and heart — which entails more study and clarity on objective moral wrong and personal, subjective involvement — is needed.

New Theological Genres

In the renewal of moral theology since Vatican II, new genres of study emerged. Liberation and justice are key virtues for several of the new theological methods. Countries suffering from extreme poverty have found Eurocentric and First World theologies inadequate for their situation. Liberation theology, feminist ethics, and environmental ethics, three of the more contemporary schools of theology, find traditional theologies do not adequately address their needs and, in some cases, aggravate their problems.

Originating in Latin America, liberation theology received its impetus from the 1968 meeting of the Conference of Latin American Bishops (CELAM) in Medellín, Colombia. The bishops issued sixteen short and concise documents that outline their stand in favor of the poor. The documents describe the conditions of the people and give a theology that supports the mandate of the church to be on the side of the poor. Documents such as those on the family, education, demographics, and the clergy are practical and bold in their stand. Latin American theologians readily followed the leadership of the bishops in developing a theology of liberation that could be easily understood by the people, many of whom are illiterate. Scripturally based, liberation theology uses the Book of Exodus and biblical themes on liberation for its theological foundation. Like the Israelites who desired to be liberated from their slavery in Egypt, the poor desire liberation from the slavery of poverty that keeps them bound in every way. In addition to liberation theology, the renewal of theology also offered a concrete framework in which the theology could be utilized. That framework is "base communities," where small groups of people meet to discuss scripture, their living situation, reflect on both, and decide on an action that can implement the call of God to liberation.

The situation of the poor demonstrated the need for a new theology that shows God is with the poor and that nourishes their faith when they feel abandoned by God. Their questions of faith stem from the injustices they suffer. Their answers come through a theology of liberation that seems capable of meeting their needs while challenging other more traditional theologies to examine their foundational premises that have allowed such dire inequalities to exist between peoples. Liberation theology gives an intellectual framework for the life situation of people but also provides a spirituality and motivation to action that place responsibility on the shoulders of the people for changing their own situation. The Vatican has examined the writings of liberation theologians and corrected those areas needing attention.[13] Recent popes have employed the basic concepts of liberation theology when they wrote on development (Paul VI), solidarity, and the option for the poor (John Paul II).

Gustavo Gutiérrez was a pioneering liberation theologian when *A Theology of Liberation* was published in 1971. Since the publication of Gutiérrez's seminal work, many other Latin American theologians, like Jon Sobrino, S.J., Leonardo Boff, José Míguez Bonino, and Juan Luis Segundo, S.J., have contributed to the theological themes of liberation and justice. Besides Latin America, liberation theologies have developed in Africa and Asia, where millions of people live in deplorable conditions.[14]

Justice not only for the poor but for minorities is redefined in liberation theologies. Women are considered a minority in countries that do not give them equal rights. Their plight has led to legal battles and has raised ethical questions on all levels of society from business to religion. Feminist ethics, a form of liberation theology, studies the ethical concerns of women in the light of church tradition. Because church tradition has kept women in a subordinate position, many women do not find traditional moral theology helpful. Feminist studies takes scripture for its source and bypasses church tradition for its foundation. Feminist theologians speak directly to the condition of women and offer theological grounding for new ways of thinking about their place before God, church, and society.

Another development in moral theology is concerned with the future of the earth. Nuclear weapons threaten the life of the earth. Technological and industrial developments mushroom in gigantic proportions, but the developments seem to take little heed of the earth's environment. Too often industrial developments cause serious environmental hazards such that people suffer from contaminated drinking water and air. Plants and animals are harmed by waste products of industry. Environmental ethics is the area of moral theology that is concerned with the ecology of the earth and the quality of life for all living beings on the earth. Theologians are trying to safeguard the earth for all life now and into the future. These theologians challenge the greed and financially driven market economies that are damaging and destroying the earth. Themes of justice, simplicity of life, and harmony of all living things bring Christians to an awareness of the fragile webs of life around them for which they are responsible. The works of Thomas Berry, Michael Dowd, Cora E. Cypser, and Eileen P. Flynn challenge Christians to environmental responsibility. This new area of ethical study shares the concern of Pope John Paul II, who has written in numerous documents about environmental concerns.

Areas of Moral Theology

The Spirit directs the church through its leaders to apply the teachings of Jesus to the contemporary world. This task is difficult because the Spirit does not "zap" answers to church and civic leaders regarding the innumerable and complex moral problems arising in different parts of the world. The problems are more complex because of the diverse cultures whose traditions must be considered in working out moral solutions. Today scholars still respond to the call of the Spirit and the challenge of Vatican II to retrieve a scriptural basis for morality and generate a renewed approach to moral dilemmas and indeed to the moral life. All areas of moral theology are responding to the call for renewal: foundational principles, sexual ethics, social ethics, medical ethics, and business ethics.

The church uses the moral principles that have been discussed in this book as guides when it enters specific areas of study. At the same time the church continues to study, dialogue, and develop more adequate applications of Jesus' teachings and the church's moral principles to the new situations that arise.

Social Ethics

Relying on "the order of reason" understanding of natural law, the teaching of the church in social ethics is concerned with the good of society and each individual in it. Pope Leo XIII in 1891 set the standard for individual rights for working people, a tradition that has continued to evolve. These developments include principles for a just wage, a family wage, adequate housing, proper working conditions, respect for women in the workplace, attention to agricultural workers as well as migrant workers, the right to strike, and just arbitration. The writings of each pope on the conditions of workers develop as new situations evolve.

As the twentieth century unfolded, the social teaching of the church moved beyond the concerns of individual workers and those of one country to a more global perspective in terms of economic conditions. Great emphasis has been placed on the poor, the disenfranchised, and those structures and systems that perpetuate poverty and injustice. The popes have spoken out boldly for freedom, justice, and rights of individuals. They have not hesitated to call countries and political leaders to task when moral evil is being perpetrated at the hands of dictators, political systems, and economic greed. The nuclear arms race was especially troubling to the popes, who challenged world leaders to come to terms with its threat to human life.

Several themes (see table 6) run through the social teaching of the church. One important theme is the *common good*. The common good is a moral principle to be heeded in all moral judgments of a social nature. Individual rights cannot supersede the common good of society, a principle that fights the evils of individualism and subjectivism. The church believes individuals are morally responsible for themselves and the structures of society.

The church has upheld the *principle of subsidiarity*, which Pius XI enunciated in his encyclical *Quadragesimo Anno:*

> It is a fundamental principle of social philosophy, fixed and unchangeable, that *one should not withdraw from individuals and commit to the community what they can accomplish by their own enterprise and industry.* So, too, it is an injustice and at the same time a grave evil and a disturbance of right order, to transfer to the larger and higher collectivity functions which can be performed and provided for by lesser and subordinate bodies. Inasmuch as every social activity should, by its very nature,

prove a help to members of the body social, it should never destroy or absorb them. (79)

Solidarity with those in need and suffering oppression, is a moral principle reiterated by recent popes but especially by Pope John Paul II. In *Sollicitudo Rei Socialis,* the pope defines solidarity as *"a firm and persevering determination to commit oneself to the common good; that is to say to the good of all and of each individual because we are all really responsible for all"* (38; emphasis added). The pope further states:

> The solidarity which we propose is the path to peace and at the same time to development. For world peace is inconceivable unless the world's leaders come to recognize that interdependence in itself demands the abandonment of the politics of blocs, the sacrifice of all forms of economic, military or political imperialism, and the transformation of mutual distrust into collaboration. This is precisely the act proper to solidarity among individuals and nations. (39)

Besides solidarity, the social tradition of the church emphasizes *justice* in all interpersonal and international relations. Human beings have *rights and freedoms* that must be respected. These require just structures to ensure the freedom of individuals and nations. The social teaching calls for structural and systemic change, not just conversion of individuals.

Table 6
Social Justice Principles

Common Good
Subsidiarity
Solidarity
Justice
Rights and Freedom
Peace
Respect for Life

The moral tradition of the church works for *peace* and opposes violence and war as solutions to problems because it places a high value on human life. *Evangelium Vitae,* issued in 1995, upholds the *respect for all human life* at all stages of its development, from conception to old age. The church stands in strong opposition to abortion, euthanasia, the use of human beings for experimentation, and capital punishment.

The social ethics tradition of the church is rich in its dynamic stands and lively challenge to society's power structures and leaders. The social teachings of the church build on the basic moral concepts of the tradition and develop as new moral issues surface.

Sexual Ethics

The approach to natural law based on "the order of nature" guides the church's moral tradition on sexual ethics. Sexual ethics is a much debated and volatile topic because of conflicting moral standards in society. What was unacceptable moral behavior in the 1930s, 1940s, or 1950s is now acceptable after the sexual revolution of the 1960s. In *Gaudium et Spes*, the Fathers of Vatican II addressed the multitude of moral concerns brought on by the sexual revolution. Strong support is given to committed, loving relationships in marriage, which the church sees as a state of lifelong fidelity. Marriage and family life are under attack because of divorce, economic pressures, artificial means of birth control, and societal patterns that do not support the raising of children or fidelity in marriage. By emphasizing the community of love, unity, and covenant love, Vatican II took a stand on the side of married couples.

The moral tradition of the church holds that all sexual activity is reserved to the state of marriage. Both the unity of the couple and procreation are to be considered in every sexual act and are considered inseparable ends of marriage. Offspring are to be brought into a family environment in the context of marriage, the context in which children can be properly reared and educated. Procreation is an important part of sexual morality because children are a means of sharing love generously. Their life is an expression of the love the spouses have for each other and for God. Sexual activity outside of marriage does not take account of generous outgoing love through children and compromises the dignity of the person. Premarital and extramarital sex encourage promiscuity and show a lack of respect for the person who may be used to satisfy lustful passions.

The magisterium is particularly concerned about the use of artificial means of birth control. After his election, Paul VI was mandated to complete the work of Vatican II on marriage and family life. This he did through the encyclical *Humanae Vitae,* which focused on married love, responsible parenthood, natural family planning, and the problems of artificial means of birth control. Abortion was strongly condemned in this document and again in the 1995 encyclical *Evangelium Vitae* of Pope John Paul II. Respect for life and respect for all persons are moral principles that undergird all teachings on sexual ethics.

Medical Ethics

The basic moral principle of respect for life applies in equally strong terms to medical issues. Biological research and medical technology have advanced in extraordinary ways during the past twenty-five years. Breakthroughs in a number of the branches of science have contributed to new developments in the art of healing. Radiology and computer science are but two branches of science that have enabled medical personnel to perform surgeries and cure diseases previously impossible to remedy.

The research of scientists is laudatory and encouraged by the church. However, scientific development has also opened a Pandora's box of moral questions. Because something is medically possible, is it morally permissible? The church is unwilling to affirm any type of research or procedure that does not respect human life. Therefore, fetal experimentation, use of fetal tissue, and cloning of human tissue are not morally acceptable scientific procedures.

Since life is sacred from the moment of conception, abortion is considered the taking of human life, as is euthanasia near the end of life. Both abortion and euthanasia show a lack of respect for human life and are therefore forbidden. The fundamental moral principle is that God gives life, and only God can take life; human beings should not have the power to determine the life and death of any individual. Pain should be alleviated, and all reasonable procedures should be used to cure a person, but finally only God determines the length of life for each of us. Traditional teachings still apply: all ordinary means are to be used, but extraordinary means need not be used because Christians believe there is an eternal life for which this life is but a preparation.

Business Ethics

Capitalism is the financial setting for American businesses and companies. Many moral dilemmas unique to a capitalist society arise for the businessperson. Some moral issues facing the disciple of Jesus in the marketplace include: excessive competition, corporations and conscience, management practices, social responsibility, the "glass ceiling," sexual harassment, privacy, union rights and responsibilities, price fixing, investment, family welfare, fair wages, and setting standards. This fist full of issues shows the wide range of dilemmas on the desk of the CEO and nearly everyone in the business world. Caught between survival and success, many businesspeople strive to provide quality products and services as well as responsible care for their employees. While some bend the rules of government and find loopholes that enable them to succeed, others work hard and honestly to make decisions in conscience that reflect social responsibility, concern for the environment, justice for workers, and a right means to earn a profit.

Basic moral principles regarding the human person and workers have been spelled out in the traditional teachings of the church. The U.S. bishops issued a document on the economy in 1986, *Economic Justice for All,* that gave moral guidance to people making economic decisions. The bishops spelled out six moral principles in the document:

1. Every economic decision and institution must be judged in light of whether it protects or undermines the dignity of the human person.

2. Human dignity can be realized and protected only in community.

3. All people have a right to participate in the economic life of society.

4. All members of society have a special obligation to the poor and vulnerable.

5. Human rights are the minimum conditions for life in community.

6. Society as a whole, acting through public and private institutions, has the moral responsibility to enhance human dignity and protect human rights.

The moral principles of the pastoral letter give an overview of the vision of economic life that must be translated into concrete measures. Unemployment, poverty and efforts to eradicate poverty, economic policies, loss of family farms, and the rights of workers are some of the areas addressed by the bishops. The pastoral letter calls for a conversion of heart. While we in the United States are richly blessed, we are also sinners who

> are not always wise or loving or just;...for all our amazing possibilities, we are incompletely born, wary of life, and hemmed in by fears and empty routines. We are unable to entrust ourselves fully to the living God, and so we seek substitute forms of security in material things, in power, in indifference, in popularity, in pleasure. (23)

The pastoral letter challenges people involved in the U.S. economy not only to think differently but also to act differently (25). New types of choices must be made that reflect religious beliefs and decisions of conscience in the secular marketplace. "We cannot separate what we believe from how we act in the marketplace and the broader community, for this is where we make our primary contribution to the pursuit of economic justice" (25). Conversion is required if the Word of God is to reach every level of life from the marketplace to the study of moral theology itself.

Conclusion

Vatican II called for renewal of all areas of the church, including moral theology. The direction for renewal is to retrieve Jesus as the norm of the moral life and to form moral character, a daunting task. Scripture and the traditions of the church are to ground moral teachings and the study of moral theologians. Theologians strive to meet this challenge as they study and apply the church's teachings to our world with its numerous and complex moral problems. Each of us is also challenged to find ways, consistent with scripture and tradition, to apply our beliefs and moral convictions.

Notes

1. Henrik Ibsen, *A Doll's House* (1879), 147.
2. Bernard Häring, *Free and Faithful in Christ,* vol 1: *General Moral Theology* (New York: Seabury Press, 1978), 289.
3. Louis Janssens, "Artificial Insemination: Ethical Considerations," *Louvain Studies* 8 (spring 1980): 13.
4. John Macmurray, *Persons in Relation* (Atlantic Highlands, N.J.: Humanities Press, 1983), 17.
5. Thomas Aquinas, *Summa Theologiae,* II–II, q. 47, art. 10.

6. See Enda McDonagh, *Invitation and Response: Essays in Christian Moral Theology* (New York: Sheed and Ward, 1972), 53.

7. Raymond F. Collins, *Christian Morality: Biblical Foundations* (South Bend, Ind.: University of Notre Dame Press, 1986), 1–3.

8. Richard M. Gula, *Reason Informed by Faith* (New York: Paulist Press, 1989), 239–40.

9. See Vincent P. Mainelli, ed., *Official Church Teaching: Social Justice* (Wilmington, N.C.: McGrath, 1978), 210.

10. See ibid., 255.

11. Gula, *Reason*, 233ff.

12. John A. Gallagher, *Time Past, Time Future: An Historical Study of Catholic Moral Theology* (New York: Paulist Press, 1990), 204.

13. See *Instruction on Christian Freedom and Liberation* (Congregation for the Doctrine of the Faith, 1986).

14. Deane William Ferm, *Profiles in Liberation* (Mystic, Conn.: Twenty-Third Publications, 1988).

CONCLUSION

Studying moral theology is a daunting challenge. Difficult as the search for moral truth and goodness has been throughout the centuries, the search continues to challenge us even today. This book has outlined several themes that guide the learner and the believer in living the moral life and in the study of moral theology.

Basic to any understanding of Catholic morality is an understanding of its person-oriented approach. Vatican II restored a Christocentric approach based on the life of Jesus. In the scriptures we find the words, actions, life, and death of Jesus, who is our norm for the moral life. This approach to morality begins with the person of Jesus and continues its search for moral truth and goodness in human persons. We are creatures made in the image of God and are called to continue the mission of Jesus.

Discipleship is a second theme that arises from the personal relationship each believer has with Jesus. Once we encounter the Lord in our lives, we are invited and drawn — even "freely compelled" — to become his disciple, to follow his way both in mind and heart. This attraction is but the beginning of a lifelong journey in moral living as a disciple of Jesus. No greater challenge exists than to "put on the mind and heart of Jesus"; the challenge is peace-filled and joyous, but also arduous and demanding.

Our efforts in discipleship we call conversion, a third theme of this book. We encounter ourselves at every turn with desires and attractions to other journeys that appear less arduous and demanding. Conversion turns us from the individualistic and materialistic allurements of modern culture to focus once again on the person of Jesus and his call to live a moral life.

Disciples quickly realize that we do not journey alone — Jesus' own Spirit is with us and is in the community of believers. This community of faith is the church, whose leaders and members guide and accompany us on the road of discipleship.

Through the different eras of history, the Holy Spirit has guided the church in its efforts to lead believers in their journey of faith.

Each new era of church history stands on the shoulders of the faithful who have gone before, some of whom paid for their faith with their life's blood. Men and women of high intellectual, moral, and spiritual caliber have served the church through their gifts. Some have been prophets, kings, patriarchs, hierarchy, and laity. These have helped to formulate wise decisions that serve as the backbone of moral theology to this day. Practices that served the church well in one period of history have yielded to new thought and new practices to meet the needs of believers in new eras. At times the church became entrenched because of entanglements by individuals and institutions in political and economic situations. At those times sinful human nature showed itself in leaders and followers of Christ. In retrospect one can see the leadership of the Spirit that corrected these situations. Throughout the church's history we can trace a belief in one God, the community's efforts to achieve the primacy of love, a desire for truth and justice, and the yearning for compassion and forgiveness modeled by Jesus.

The loving disciple strives to live a moral life and so to put on the mind and heart of Jesus Christ. Such effort discloses a fourth theme of this book: formation of moral character. Character defines who we are as persons. Traits of character are wed to our being, particularly when we speak of moral character. Integrity, truth, courage, goodness, love, and compassion are significant traits of moral character that flow from one's basic character. Since Catholic moral theology is person-oriented, the primary goal is to form a moral character modeled on the person of Jesus. We learn this best from the example of other believers and most especially from the modeling of moral values given by those we love. It is not sufficient to perform certain acts or do specific deeds like those of Jesus; rather these acts are to express the moral tenor and character of the disciple. The disciple allows the self to be shaped by the Master's love and to reveal love for the Master through moral dispositions, patterns of thought, actions, ways of loving, attitudes, and emotive leanings. Like discipleship, the formation of moral character is a lifelong journey.

The disciple ultimately agrees that Jesus is the Word of eternal life. To understand Catholic morality means to understand Jesus and discipleship through putting on the mind and heart of Jesus.

ELIZABETH WILLEMS, S.S.N.D., a professor of moral theology at Notre Dame Seminary in New Orleans, earned her doctoral degree at Marquette University and completed graduate degrees at the University of Chicago and Mundelein College. As a member of the School Sisters of Notre Dame who was raised in Cologne, Minnesota, she taught in North Dakota, Iowa, and Minnesota.

OF RELATED INTEREST

HOW TO READ THE OLD TESTAMENT
0-8245-0540-9; $14.95 pb

HOW TO READ THE NEW TESTAMENT
0-8245-0541-7; $14.95 pb

HOW TO READ CHURCH HISTORY
From the Beginnings to the 15th Century
0-8245-0722-3; $16.95 pb

HOW TO READ CHURCH HISTORY
From the Reformation to the Present
0-8245-0908-0; $18.95 pb

HOW TO UNDERSTAND CHURCH AND MINISTRY IN THE UNITED STATES
0-8245-1468-8; $16.95 pb

HOW TO UNDERSTAND THE SACRAMENTS
0-8245-1026-7; $16.95 pb

Please support your local bookstore, or call 1-800-395-0690.
For a free catalog, please write us at
THE CROSSROAD PUBLISHING COMPANY
370 LEXINGTON AVENUE, NEW YORK, NY 10017

We hope you enjoyed Understanding Catholic Morality. *Thank you for reading it.*

crossroad